TUNE UP YOUR
CAREER

Tips & Cautions for Peak Performance
in the Workplace

CHRIS FONTANELLA

ILLUMIFY
MEDIA.COM

Tune Up Your Career

Copyright © 2023 by Chris Fontanella

Published by
Illumify Media Global
www.IllumifyMedia.com
"Let's bring your book to life!"

Paperback ISBN: 978-1-959099-07-9

Typeset by Jen Clark
Cover design by Debbie Lewis

Printed in the United States of America

To my mom, a never-ending source of support and love, and the person who instilled in me an appreciation for the arts.

CONTENTS

FOREWORD

BY MIKE KELLY, CPA (INACTIVE), PARTNER, CONEXUS
RECRUITING

Twenty years ago, I lost two recruiting searches in two months to Chris. I was so impressed, I had to meet him, so I reached out and we had lunch. From that lunch it was obvious why Chris was one of the best in the business. His ability to build real relationships quickly with both client and candidate was tangible. Over the years we stayed in touch to discuss what was going on in the recruiting business, in the economy, and to spit ball business ideas. Over the last thirty years in the people business, he has not only been incredibly successful as an individual contributor, leader but also entrepreneur.

I wish I had read *Tune-Up Your Career* when I started my professional career. This book does a great job of focusing the reader on both personal and professional success. It helps you build a tactical framework to move forward, overcome challenges, and take ownership of your career path. Personal and professional success are not always tied to each other, and rarely do you achieve them in straight line, but by reading this book, you are significantly better prepared for the roller-coaster ride we all face.

INTRODUCTION

In my book, *Jump-Start Your Career,* I address those who are about to commence their life of employment: recent graduates from college or vocational school and also those who are opting to enter the workforce right after high school.

The book offers advice on topics such as finding your calling (a word I use interchangeably with career), mapping out your "territory" of exploration (i.e, drafting a plan for what you want to do for a living), setting ambitious goals (pocket-sized dreams are too small), seeing unseen worlds (possibilities others cannot imagine), realizing achievements depend on the contributions of others (reaching career goals is never a solo effort), expecting obstacles (the streets that lead to noteworthy careers are strewn with challenges), remembering careers develop over time (you can't rush your way into a great career), being willing to start at the bottom (starting *there* prepares you for being at the top), letting your work speak for itself (accomplishments are their own reward; let others praise your efforts), and never minimizing your uniqueness (any job that does not allow you to be you is not the job for you).

If you have just started your life of employment and have picked up *this* book, it might be a good idea to read *that* book first.

Tune Up Your Career presupposes you're an employee with some tenure; you are further down the road. You have worked ten to twenty years and have dated or married, so to speak, a number of employers. You have paid some dues and climbed the corporate ladder, somewhat, whatever that means. You know the drill, and maybe what it is like to be chained to your work or to "work for the man," used here, nonchauvinistically, to mean you work for someone besides yourself.

Still, despite having some years under your belt, perhaps you find it hard to navigate the corporate world, and your career engine just doesn't seem to have the oomph it used to. The evolution of your working life may have slowed or, worse yet, stalled.

Maybe your career has not turned out the way you planned: the title, the money, and the respect you think you deserve are absent. And it lacks a sense of purpose. You imagined it differently and hoped it would be so. Yet you can still envision it being different. The picture of what you'd like it to be pops up in your mind on occasion. But all forward movement has stopped. You feel stuck and are struggling to make the best of the "system" in which you work.

Work has worked you over. You feel like a jack-in-the-box who can't seem to get—or think—outside the box.

Whether you like it or not, being employed means you are part of a capitalistic system (it's the box "Jack" lives in), and your survival depends on active, intelligent participation within it. Since "money makes the world go round"—and you have to work to earn it—you might as well make the most of the time you spend inside that framework. For work to work for you, you must learn to function better within that structure. That's just the way it is.

To what can we compare the framework of work? To what is "work life" analogous?

A couple comparisons come to mind: a maze and a machine.

Making your way through your work world can be like meandering through a maze. As a mouse scampers here and there in search of cheese, so you hasten through your labyrinth seeking payment ("cheddar") for your time and effort. Each day you enter and put your best paw forward, hoping the "rewards" keep coming. But finding and obtaining those rewards is no easy task—navigating corporate corridors is challenging, and office halls are often strewn with "traps." You are sure to step on one if you wander in an aimless fashion; a relaxed ramble through your work maze is not advised.

A machine—an apparatus applying mechanical power and having several parts, each with a specific function—is not an uncommon metaphor for the workplace. It conjures images of an industrial-like, hammer-pounding, crank-shit-out, just-do-your-job environment that reminds us we are all, in one way or another, assigned a function to help keep the big wheel of the economic market turning. Each day, consciously or unconsciously, you play a part in that production: you provide a service to a client, manufacture a widget, pontificate on talk radio, tend bar, manage money, flip houses, or scan groceries. Fill in the blank with whatever it is you do. Most workers, at one time or another, feel like a cog in the wheel of industry.

Over time, if you are not careful—if you're not conscientiously managing your career—the puzzling network of paths will disorient you, and the workplace machinery will strip you of your individuality.

Part 1 of this book further explores these metaphors and serves to highlight what life is like on the inside of the maze and machine, the assumption being that for you to function better at work—for work to *not* work you over—you must have an appreciation of that environment. If you understand the nature of something, you will know better how to exist in relation to it.

The second part of the book provides tips to improve your performance within that setting. It offers "maintenance" suggestions to keep your "career engine" in tip-top shape and pointers to ensure it performs well and has the power needed to get you where you want to go.

Not all engines are the same, but all need power. In a conventional engine, a mixture of gasoline and air provide the explosiveness that moves the pistons, which then turns the crankshaft to which they are attached. Alternatively, electric vehicles use rechargeable batteries to empower the motor. Regardless of the engine type—and each is complex in its own way—both need energy for the car to function as intended.

Look at it this way: the engine is the heart of the car, the organ that pumps fuel for the car to do what it is capable of doing. Its functionality diminishes if problems develop, like oil leaks, worn-out bearings, dirty filters, bad serpentine belts, and timing issues. Left unaddressed, the problems only get worse.

Which is why cars need tune-ups, periodic maintenance sessions to make sure all parts are functioning well.

Careers—like cars—also need to be brought to the "shop" for maintenance. Problems need to be fixed before they become bigger issues. You might be saying to yourself, *I hate my job*, or *This is not the role for me*, or *Something doesn't feel right about being at this company*, or *I know I graduated with a degree in accounting, but I think I want to be a veterinarian*. These and other thoughts like them may be driving around the streets and avenues of your mind and heart. The dashboard lights of your career engine are flashing. Best to let someone take a look under the hood before it's too late.

The tips suggested in part 2 of this book assume you are overdue for a maintenance check—your career engine is sputtering or it has stalled. But it also assumes you want to fix things so it will hum again.

To that end, you will be encouraged to

- Take ownership of your career: assume complete responsibility for your life of employment.
- Consider entrepreneurship: take a hard look at whether or not you are meant to be in business for yourself.
- Take a broader view of "wrong" moves: embrace a more positive perspective about the missteps taken on your career path.
- Learn how to interpret the tea leaves in the bottom of your cup: translate (think differently about) the changes that have occurred throughout your career.
- Realize a step down can be a step up: learn to align yourself with a job that allows you to be true to yourself.

In part 3 of this book, I issue a warning about greed (presented in two different ways in chapters 8 and 9). Money is not a bad thing in and of itself. On the surface, having more of it seems better than having less of it; at least that's the way I see it. That said, an inordinate focus on obtaining it can be detrimental. There is sure to be some form of collateral damage when the love of money is an "unsleeping, ever-pacing thought," as Melville says of Ahab's obsession to kill Moby Dick.[1] Lest the maintenance tips offered be confused with suggestions for "striking it rich"—though I believe they do lead to a "wealthy" life—it seems appropriate to strike at least one cautionary note. This section ends with a parable to drive home the point that an unquenching desire for "more, more, more" can make you "poor, poor, poor."

Lastly, a feature called Spark Plugs ends each chapter, reviewing key points that can be easily referenced later and offering a few exercises that reinforce the material in the chapter. Just as a mechanic takes steps to tune up a car's engine, so, too, should you take steps to improve the performance of your career engine.

Whether you realize it or not, you are overdue for a career tune-up—it's one of those things we must do but tend to put off. Keep reading if you what to get that engine humming once again.

PART 1
WORKPLACE METAPHORS

1 MICE, MAZES, AND MANCHEGO

IMAGINE YOU ARE A MOUSE.

In a maze.

Looking for cheese.

A mouse in a maze looking for cheese has its challenges: towering walls, darkened hallways, dead ends, and the brain-rattling pitter-patter of other mouse feet echoing off the entire structure. Most mice, at one time or another, lose their way and get lost.

On top of that, there's a smell permeating the enclosure, an alluring aroma that carries them, almost against their will, like a baby lulled to a delightful dwelling of dreams, a habitat of happiness. Overcome by natural impulses, they scurry here and there in search of the seductive scent. Its fragrance fascinates the instinctive critter like a charmer hypnotizing a snake. All the mouse cares about, all it really wants is *cheese*: scrumptious, delicious, savory *cheese*.

That's some existence.

I guess it beats being a hamster on a running wheel treadmilling to destinations never reached.

The finding cheese part sounds good, though.

Lucky for me, finding cheese comes easily. Six or seven varieties fill the cheese drawer in my refrigerator, always. And when I reward myself, like after closing a business deal, I walk straight to that drawer. No circuitous routes to figure out, no labyrinthine layout to navigate—just a simple stroll from point A to point B.

The more deals I close, the more I celebrate. And my celebrations always include cold libations, room-temp cheese, and RITZ Crackers, because "everything tastes great when it sits on a RITZ." I believe it. Put a piece of cheese on one and fuhgeddaboudit. You can't beat it.

All types of cheese work for me, like creamy Monterey jack, sharp aged cheddar, and briny feta. Some days I prefer nutty Parmesan or milky mozzarella; other days I lean toward zesty pepper jack, flavorful Manchego, or smoked Gruyère. The type doesn't matter. Nor do I care if it comes sliced, chunked, shredded, or grated; even cheese spreads are delicious, like WisPride, a smooth blend of cheddar and port wine. Indulging myself this way is like getting a pat on the back for a job well done.

Who could fault a mouse for sniffing his way through the puzzle-like structure until he finds some?

Years back, Dr. Spencer Johnson wrote a quaint tale entitled *Who Moved My Cheese?* about two mice and two "little people," as they're called in the book, looking for cheese in a maze. All four are similar in that "every morning, they each put on their jogging suits and running shoes, [leave] their little homes, and [race] out into the maze looking for their favorite cheese."[1]

The hungry foursome—Sniff, Scurry, Hem, and Haw—get lucky. They hit the mother lode and find the cheese of their dreams, what they assume is a lifetime supply. Overjoyed with their discovery, they nibble and nosh until their bellies are full, then return home squeaking about their good fortune.

They develop a habit of returning to the station where they first found the cheese, assuming it will be there every day. Until the day it is not. The cheese gets moved to another section in the maze. Not one shred could be found in its usual location.

These "lab rats" must now decide what to do. Do they remain where they first found cheese, hoping it will be placed there again and again, or do they venture out, searching the maze to find a new batch?

Spencer's mice each respond differently. Sniff and Scurry, who "noticed the supply of cheese had been getting smaller every day," laced up their running shoes and went on the hunt. Hem and Haw, who "had not been paying attention to the small changes that had been taking place each day," complained, sat in disbelief, and made no productive moves.[2] "While Sniff and Scurry had quickly moved on, Hem and Haw continued to hem and haw."[3]

My response would vary: I am prone to laziness, am often uninspired, and like Hem and Haw, get comfortable, to a fault, when I have what I think I need. It doesn't take much for me to get settled in my "cage." If I am being honest, more often than not I would wait for the cheese to come to me. But then again, being a salesman, I appreciate a good hunt. Running through the maze has its rewards. I am motivated because, as we say in my household, "Everything is better with cheddar."

Like Spencer Johnson's mice, I suspect we all respond to change differently.

His parable highlights two truths: circumstances change, and survival depends on your ability to adapt.

Mice know this instinctively, and people do too. We humans are more like mice than we care to admit—the best test subjects resemble us.

Both mice and people know that life changes from one day to the next, as certain as the rising and setting of the sun. People utter, "Carpe diem," and "Live each day as if it were your last," because intuitively they know all things change. Each day brings something new, and we must make the most of it—and not whine about the shifting nature of circumstances.

The reality: you have less time than you think, and by being idle, you waste more of it than you should. Best to adapt and move on.

Some days are good, some are bad, and some are the "same old same old," but the DNA of *every* day contains uncertainty— that vague feeling of not knowing what each day holds, that something might be coming around the corner, that change is on its way and can appear at any moment—a nagging thought wandering your mind like a restless spirit roaming a haunted house. Some peer into crystal balls to find out what it may be, hoping that the shapeless reality will step out of the mist that enshrouds it, hoping to learn what the future holds. But it is impossible to predict the future, which eludes us all. The unknown makes itself known in its own time. Only then does the "yet to be defined" get a "definition."

Uncertainty is unsettling. It disturbs the status quo of one's day-to-day existence. But it also reminds us of the inevitability of change and the need to adapt, which is a good thing. Living in a state of ambiguity can be hard, but once the "unknown" steps out from the shadows—and we understand what we are dealing with—then we can make decisions. "Uncertainty," says Ram Charan in his book *The Attacker's Advantage,* "is not something to fear, but rather something to immerse yourself in, because in it lie the possibilities you can combine to create something new and immensely valuable."[4]

At times, careers lack clarity and certainty. Out of the blue, everything changes: the boss you love gets the ax; a private equity firm acquires the company you work for; the promotion you hoped for goes to your coworker; a 35 percent workforce reduction occurs, and you are part of it; or management outsources your job to another country.

Employment life—and life in general—is dynamic, not static. "To imagine that things in this life [and in your career] are always to remain as they are," says Cervantes in *Don Quixote*, "is to indulge in an idle dream."[5] Sorry to be the one to tell you, but in this life nothing ever stays the same, including your job.

After making the unlikely, unpopular decision *not* to be a minister, I had no idea what to do with myself or what direction my "career" would take. Dreams and desires danced in my head like the Sugar Plum Fairy and the three windup dolls in *The Nutcracker*, but I felt lost. My future was as uncertain as what's going to happen in the year 2065.

And my first postministry job left me uninspired; managing a vault operation for a bank lacked pizzaz. My office—part cage, part maze—had a twelve-inch-thick steel door entrance, four walls, and aisles you walked up and down in search of bonds and securities for customers, like a mouse searching for cheese. When you entered the vault, you signed in. When you exited, you signed out. No exceptions. Company policy demanded the door always remain locked. When you left for the day, you felt like Stuart Little on an adventure in the "real world."

Quite the cheese-less existence, I must say.

But it taught me about mazes and how to maneuver through them, and that not all mice are like Spencer's, who found cheese on their first expedition.

A couple years into the job, the "big cheese" (the boss) told all the hardworking mice in the office how important we were to the organization. He said upper management noticed our impressive contributions to the bank's bottom line and assured us we were "secure" in our jobs—a pat on the back but not the kind I would give myself. RITZ crackers and cheese seemed in order.

But my little mouse heart pulsed with joy knowing I could "bank" on a steady supply of cheese (my salary), at least for the near future. Elated, I returned to my cage-like vault.

But fate waved its baton, summoning life's orchestra to play music in a different time signature, one more complex and a bit offbeat. The solemn sounds seemed to whisper the following: today cannot be yesterday, yesterday cannot be today, and tomorrow will be tomorrow.

Then "tomorrow" spoke. Shortly after the big cheese's announcement—literally one week later—he delivered a different message to the staff. He regretted to inform us that another bank had bought the corporate trust division, of which we were a part. I wondered, *Shouldn't management consult me before making such a decision since it was going to impact my life?* And *Was my best interest of no interest to them?* I came to learn, that's just not how it works. Decisions like that are made without my input.

And I also learned that nothing good follows a sentence that starts with "I regret to inform you."

My mind raced faster than Speedy Gonzales: *Wait . . . what? I thought management appreciated our hard work. Is this our reward? What happened between last week and today?*

The "rat pack" was given two options: join the acquiring bank or lose your job. No immediate pressure, though; they gave us a year to decide. (This happened in the late 1980s. Today you would not be afforded this luxury of time.)

My cheese had moved, just like Spencer's book says it would.

Management at the bank communicated a clear message: you could stay or leave, but if you stayed, your job would be in Minnesota. Yup! Minnesota. Of all places!

How would you respond?

Would you follow the cheese and relocate to the land of ten thousand Lakes? Minnesota knows a thing or two about cheese; Land O'Lakes has been there since 1921. It could be nice.

Another option: jump ship like rats fleeing the *Titanic*. In other words, view the change as an opportunity to abandon one course of action for another.

Management gave a one-year notice regarding the impending changes. That's like the captain on the *Titanic* telling you water has filled the galley, a signal flare has been fired, an SOS has been transmitted, and the musicians have ceased playing their instruments. Nothing would be—could be—the same, ever again. To think things would remain as they were would be foolishness. Or as Tess Vigeland, former host of Public Radio's *Marketplace*, puts it in her book *Leap: Leaving a Job with No Plan B to Find the Career and Life You Really Want*, "Here's the thing to remember: the safety we build around ourselves is, by and large, an illusion."[6]

The question then becomes, How do you react when those unexpected moments happen?

The bank felt like home to me, and I knew Minnesota would not. The *familiar* is warm and comfortable; the *unknown*, not so much. But that doesn't mean I should remain in my comfort zone and not venture into uncharted territory. Maybe you've had similar feelings about your job or the company you work for; maybe not.

Everyone has different ideas on what home means. I associate it with my parents, my brother, my cousins, my friends, and family traditions. When I close my eyes, I envision family members in the rec room of my parents' house having drinks and antipasto—a platter of cheeses, cured meats, and other tasty morsels. We congregate at the bar, a custom-made work of art created by Tippy Larkin, a carpenter from the neighborhood. Its craftmanship has stood the test of time: its condition shows no wear and tear from the day he put it in some forty-plus years ago. Sitting there is like being at church, where the faithful receive communion, though we serve a much stiffer "sacrament."

My parents still live in that house, and family and friends still gather around in fellowship, drinking from a communal cup of memories and shared experiences. My childhood home serves as a repository for these and other recollections, like the Jimi Hendrix poster behind my bedroom door, like the times my buddy tapped on my window at one in the morning to "smoke a bone," like my years of teenage angst, like the days trapped inside the house because of a punishment I *earned*, and a host of other mental mementos I prefer to keep private.

The walls in a home speak to you, even when you're away from it. Like during my college years when I first experienced homesickness.

New Jersey can't be compared to Oklahoma, nor can college be compared to home. On Sunday mornings I sat in my dorm room—a colorless and cold cinder block cage—reminded of Mom's Sunday gravy, a simmering, aromatic pot of tomato sauce loaded with meatballs, braciola, and sausage. Later in the day, I would succumb to memories of Anthony's Pizzeria, where the aroma from the ovens greeted you in the alley leading to its entrance. The smells of my childhood were as real as the concrete enclosure I called "home" for four years. And relief only came during spring break, summer break, and holidays.

Luckily, Oklahoma had an alternative: biscuits and gravy, a white sauce made with flour and some sort of fat, like butter or pan drippings from sausage or bacon. *This* gravy, if made properly, contained sausage, a scant reminder of what could be found *in* my mom's sauce and *on* Anthony's pizzas. But biscuits and gravy were only a *reminder* of home.

They say children of military personnel find it difficult to make themselves at home. At any time, their parents, those self-sacrificing patriots dedicated to protecting our country, may be asked to transfer to one of 450 to 500 military bases in the United States or one of the 750 in foreign lands. They have no choice and must go where assigned.

As time goes by, the children, familiar with the drill, learn that boxes should be packed and unpacked with emotionless efficiency. Family get-togethers, party time in the rec room, and neighbors you've known for years, like Tippy Larkin, rarely exist. For an army brat, home is a return address on an envelope. They live in a *house*, not a *home*. One phone call can disturb and disrupt their dwelling.

Similarly, in today's workplace, you may never feel settled in your job: at any time a transfer can happen. Behind the scenes, corporations discuss mergers and acquisitions, divestitures, leveraged buyouts, and takeovers—all with the potential to trigger a life-altering, unanticipated moment in your life. Don't take it personally: business clouds drop rain on everyone without passion or prejudice. They know neither hierarchy, nor compensation bracket, nor tenure. Their drops fall on all.

I decided against Minnesota and left the bank, even though it felt like home, sort of.

Call me naïve, but at the time (I was twenty-eight years old), I did not think too much about the existence of other "mazes." But shortly thereafter, I found one in the *a-mazing* world of staffing, an industry that allowed me to find jobs for people, and one I never would have come across if not for the bank's decision to sell its corporate trust division, an event I never planned for or marked on my calendar.

If the bank had not "moved my cheese," I would not have found my new "home."

Far from unique, this kind of thing happens all the time. Employers make decisions that impact you: they downsize the company (make the maze smaller); they acquire other companies (make the maze bigger); they consolidate company operations (and in the process, decide which mice stay and which mice go); and sometimes they determine you're just not the right mouse for the job (e.g., you're a Mickey, but they need a Minnie or vice versa).

Disorienting, to say the least. No wonder mice in mazes get discombobulated.

Maze disorientation can paralyze, but mousetraps maim and kill. As you scamper around your maze, beware of the traps strewn about.

One day, as I sniffed my way down a familiar corridor, head down and nose to the floor, I came upon one of these limb-shattering, life-ending mousetrap devices. The word *Allegiance* was stamped on all sides.

The contraption did not appear dangerous or deadly. In fact, I found it attractive: it had shiny coils and bars and an aromatic nugget of cheese perched on a silver tray. The word *Allegiance* displayed on its side made me curious, but I did not take the bait and was left pondering the importance of loyalty. Later I recalled the following:

A long time ago, a son approached his mother and father to let them know his plans to propose to the girl of his dreams. "I'm in love, I'm in love, and I want the whole world to know it," he told them. With each passing day, his parents saw his passion and enthusiasm for the young lady grow. But being older and wiser, and knowing the rarity of "true love," they felt obligated to assess the extent of his love for her. (They had an appropriate sense of allegiance to their son.)

They asked if he had considered her faults, flaws, and idiosyncrasies. Did he see more than her charming looks, coquettish smile, and perfumed personality? Could he appreciate the wonderful yet inscrutable nature of a woman? Married over forty years themselves, they were well aware of the ups and downs of marriage.

Persuaded by their son's youthful exuberance—and the look of love in his eyes—they gave their blessing but were concerned he seemed blinded by love.

Similarly, in the late 1970s, a few thousand San Franciscans fell blindly and madly in love with someone who promised to give them a blessing, if they swore loyalty to him. No one could have imagined what the Reverend Jim Jones, charismatic cult leader who preached a message of Christian socialism, would have required from his parishioners.

Jones, like all self-aggrandizing cult leaders, claimed to be divine and exerted greater control over the members of his church, the Peoples Temple. And after a period of negative publicity, he felt compelled to relocate his church to a South American settlement in Jonestown, Guyana. Many of his "disciples" followed; most were never heard from again. These "believers," susceptible to Jones's suggestions, drank a cyanide-laced punch, which resulted in one of the most harrowing tragedies in American history. A stark reminder of the insidious nature of cults and the deadly consequences of blind allegiance, Jonestown admonished all to love with eyes wide open.

The catchphrase "drinking the Kool-Aid" now sarcastically denotes employees who swear allegiance to an organization at the expense of everything else—even themselves. The message to all employees is this: beware of the company that requires you to sip from the proverbial punch bowl. Your allegiance may cost more than you think.

Years back, my boss invited me to a dinner meeting at a swanky steak house in Los Angeles. As the evening progressed, I became disconcerted by her expression of love for the company by whom we were both employed.

As I enjoyed my filet mignon and au gratin potatoes, she

raved about our employer. The cadence of her speech increased as she spoke of the company with a glint in her eye. While off on a love-crazed oration of adoration, she lauded its management team, highlighted its uniqueness in the market, and in a giddy fashion joked about the likelihood of getting a divorce because she loved her job more.

For her, life boiled down to one thing: the firm. Everything and everyone else faded into a colorless background. Her effusive discourse recalled Avery Tolar, the likeable but corrupt lawyer in John Grisham's *The Firm*. Long past worrying about his law firm being a front for an organized crime family from Chicago, Tolar grew comfortable turning a blind eye, a task he found easier than wrestling with questions of ethics and morality. At some point he acquiesced and traded his soul for a lucrative career.

With the fervency of a revivalist tent preacher, my former boss pled with me to surrender myself into the ever-loving arms of the company she worshipped and adored. Her words filled the room but left my heart empty. Her appeal clamored and clanked like a steel ball in a pinball machine. I loved the company too but had no plans of swearing allegiance to an organization that required proof of devotion through soul sacrifice. A trap by any other name is still a trap. I resigned shortly thereafter.

Mousetrap designers eventually realized how the mice started to avoid the old spring-loaded versions, and thought a more "humane" product would appeal to a market segment that held disdain for the neck-breaking *snap* of the original. Redesigning the old model could create a new revenue stream. As they say, build a better mousetrap, and the world will beat a path to your door.

So they did, and the new version looked nothing like the old: no shiny springs, coils, or bars, and no silver platter on which to showcase cheese. Just a transparent mat with a clear, sticky substance all over it, unnoticeable but just as effective.

Heck, some mice got stuck and remained so for years before they realize they'd stepped on it. And written on it were the words *Golden Handcuffs*.

Its adhesive makes mice feel comfortable in the same spot. The desire they once had to hunt for cheese gets replaced with a nonchalant I-will-take-what-I-get attitude. The promise of a future supply keeps them fixed in one spot—the trap's glue prohibits making any moves whatsoever. To free themselves, they must relinquish their guarantee of future cheese installments. But what cheese-loving creature would do that? Only a few brave mice will gnaw off a limb to be free.

I know many who opted to "stick" with a company to cash in on its promises. Over the years, I attempted to free mice from these glue traps, all to no avail. Equity, options, and year-end bonuses handcuff them to the organization. They find it impossible to leave, even though I tell them golden handcuffs are handcuffs nonetheless.

Once I stepped onto one of these traps. In my mind it made sense to wait for my "reward" because it allowed me to walk away with enough "cheddar" to create my own maze, that is, start my own business. Each mouse must put their cheese allotment on the scale, weigh it, and determine if staying put makes sense. From what I have seen, however, most mice feel trapped by this promise and let other opportunities pass them by. And the reward never seems worth what was sacrificed to obtain it.

A final word of advice to all maze-running mice: beware of losing yourself in the maze. It can happen.

In *Harry Potter and the Goblet of Fire*, Hogwarts (a training school for wizards) hosts the legendary event known as the Triwizard Tournament, where three wizard schools meet to take part in a series of magical contests. In the final challenge, the participants must find the Triwizard Cup located at the center of the Triwizard Maze. For the winner, everlasting glory awaits.

But meandering through the maze to find the cup is no easy task. Tall hedges prevent a clear line of sight, and other challenges include Blast-Ended Skrewts, giant spiders, and Boggarts, the term J.K. Rowling uses for run-of-the-mill bogeymen.

Before the contest begins, Hogwarts's headmaster, Albus Dumbledore, offers the contestants a brief word of caution, saying, "People change in the maze. Be very wary; you could just lose yourself along the way."[7]

Mazes have a way of disorienting you, even to the point of not remembering who you are.

At one point in the competition, a disoriented Harry Potter must choose between helping a fellow contestant ensnared in the maze or claiming victory. The cup was close at hand. If he ignored the plight of his rival, victory would be his. Instead, Harry chose to backtrack and rescue his competitor. Doing right meant more to him than being crowned champion. In acting selflessly, Harry remained true to himself.

Career mazes are challenging and difficult to get through. Life within them can be unpredictable. You never really know what will happen one day to the next. At times they can be dangerous. Traps lie throughout; some "blind" you to realities that exist outside work, and others cause you to get "stuck," restricting you from potential tailor-made opportunities. You can lose your sense of direction and your sense of self in the maze. You can get so turned around that you no longer see what is really important and stop being true to yourself. Even so, one need only remember that mazes have exits. At times they may be hard to find, but they exist nonetheless.

SPARK PLUGS

- Whether you like it or not, being an employee is like being a mouse in a maze looking for cheese.
- "Cheese" is your reward for the work you do. How do you like to be rewarded? Some want to be rewarded with recognition. Others want respect. Others prefer monetary considerations. What about you? List on a note card five things that represent "cheese" to you.
- Work circumstances change all the time; survival depends on your ability to adapt. Unexpected moments will happen throughout your career. Think about the changes that have occurred in your life and at your place(s) of employment over the last five to ten years. Did you miss any opportunities to adapt? What would you have done differently?
- Remember: changing circumstances create opportunities, and adaptation is the key to survival.
- Mazes contain traps, so watch your step. List on a note card five kinds of "traps" you have noticed at your place(s) of employment.
- Do not allow the dangers and difficulties of a maze to change you. Be true to yourself. If you lose your way or lose yourself in the process, stop and begin to search for an exit. They may be hard to find, but they exist nonetheless.

2 WELCOME TO THE MACHINE

"Welcome to the Machine" is a Pink Floyd song that warns about the money-grubbing tendency of the music industry and its record producers. Unable to cope within that type of business atmosphere, one of Floyd's band members eventually suffered a mental collapse, highlighting the mauling nature of the "machine," a familiar trope for the workplace.

Tom Peters, client service manager for a multinational consulting firm, was likewise "mauled" by the machine. At first he enjoyed his role. But over time the demands of the job got to him. Sixty-five cold calls per day, twenty-five face-to-face meetings per month, revenue targets, and sales activity reporting—it all weighed on him. And a task-oriented manager intolerant of excuses only exasperated the situation.

Over an extended period of time, the pressure became too much to bear. Tom ended up in the hospital; he had had a nervous breakdown. The machine had gobbled him up and spit him out. The demand of being machine-like in his job ran contrary to his natural disposition.

At this point in your career, more than likely you are aware of the machine-like nature of corporate America and workplaces in general. When queried, employees often say they feel like a cog in a wheel toiling away, a servant whose purpose is to increase a company's profitability, only to be left feeling anonymous and dispensable. If allowed, the "machine" will manhandle you and rob you of your sense of uniqueness and distinction.

Let me tell you a story about someone who felt that way . . . and then did something about it.

Simon entered the elevator and pushed the button for the eighteenth floor. Several others filed in mechanically. All were headed to the same floor.

He tried to calculate the number of times he had made this ho-hum ascent to work for an employer he no longer believed in and a job that had dwindled in meaning. But this time, the trip up bristled with a mixture of hopefulness and determination because he would be taking a bold step to start his own company, ironically on the same floor as his old job.

Starting something new always felt that way to him, both scary and exciting.

And while he hoped this would be the beginning of something different, a nagging apprehension pestered his thoughts, like a maddening mosquito on a sultry summer day—perhaps some lingering residue from his last job, with a company which we'll call Unlimited Resources, or just the jaded outlook he had cultivated over what it meant to have a "career."

Everyone avoided eye contact, and the atmosphere in the elevator pulsed in a typical don't-look-at-me manner. Because it was early, a little before six a.m., those who entered after him looked like they labored to shed their morning slumber. Simon wondered if there was more to it. Postured militaristically, everyone appeared robotic, Borg-like reflections staring back from the metallic elevator doors. The surrounding air had a steely, programmed feel to it.

Disregarding their droid-like demeanor, Simon opted instead to tune in to the smooth-sounding instrumental jazz music piping through the speaker system, sounds which transported him into a state of reminiscence. For as long as he could remember, elevators had had that effect on him. For Simon, those oft-ignored innocuous sounds fostered reflection and instilled calm.

The button for the third floor lit up, and a *ping* echoed throughout the structure. A quick thought sprinted across his mind: "Corporate America: a machine made of men and women."

Memories of his first day of work at his old firm came to mind. A younger image of himself emerged: sharply dressed, self-assured, a bit naïve, but eager to succeed.

Ping. Floor four.

Simon ignored the elevator's call for attention and continued in contemplation.

Ping. Floor five. The elevator stopped, and its doors opened.

In walked a stylishly dressed, professional-looking female. Her dress, white with red polka dots, was complimented by perfectly matched three-inch heels. Her lipstick accentuated the color of the intoxicating array of circles on her dress that he now stared at. She reminded him of a former manager at a company where he once worked. She'd made a lasting impression on Simon because she was kind to everyone, always had a pleasant demeanor, and managed her team effectively. He wished to emulate her balanced, competent, yet caring managerial style.

Memories like this grounded Simon. They offered abatement from the ferocity of the lion's den he lived in at work and moored him to the shoreline of his humanity and softened the harshness of his daily grind, that mechanical churning of office life, which over time can drub one's soul with a sense of irrelevance.

He appreciated the effects of time—how it can break one's strength, cause one to grow feeble, diminish one's individuality, and make it hard to stand out among the crowd. If left unattended, the fire in one's heart dims, its amber warmth and glow fades, its embers spit out random flickers, reminders of yesterday's evaporating passions.

To salvage a few scraps of self-respect, Simon had resigned from his former employer. He'd had too much dignity to stay. He'd felt like a square peg being forced into a round hole. By the end of his employment there, he had started to shed the company's orthodox patterns and press beyond the cookie-cutter dimensions of how they wanted things to be done. He saw things differently and had needed an outlet to be true to himself.

The ping for the sixth floor interrupted his philosophical musings. He should be thinking about the new company he was about to start anyway. Stumbling down memory lane could wait.

Simon tended to see things from a different perspective, which stemmed from double majoring in philosophy and English literature. He loved learning about what made people tick, hence his appreciation of philosophy. But he also enjoyed literary classics, which featured brilliantly developed characters who embodied the full spectrum of humanity in all its glory— the good, the bad, and the ugly.

Even though he had found his way into a career in professional services, he never defined himself strictly as a "businessman," concerned only with dollars and cents. His education prevented him from accepting simplistic definitions of people, ones fraught with limitations. In his mind, a business professional should be so much more than a person who thinks only about business.

As the elevator made its way up the next few floors, he could not help but think how his last job had taken a lot out of him. Three years in had left him feeling awash in what Aldous Huxley would call an "indistinguishable sameness." By the time he left, only a few offbeat, unconventional employees remained. Some might say they kept time to the beat of a different drum; others might call them rebels.

As the organization grew, hiring had degenerated into identifying like-minded pedigreed professionals. And with each new hire, a gnawing sense of unimportance had crept into Simon's soul, which caused him to question management and the means they used to accomplish company goals.

While working at Unlimited Resources, he never told anyone how he felt about this lest an unwelcome spotlight be pointed at him. That sort of attention might highlight skills and credentials he lacked opposed to the talents and gifts he possessed. So he kept his nose to the grindstone and let his revenue production speak for itself. It is hard to argue with the numbers, he thought, and putting good numbers on the board seemed to keep one in good stead with management.

Unlimited Resources valued revenue production. Aside from that, they only cared about whether or not an employee adhered to the gospel preached by management, better known as the "Eight Steps of Sales Success." Its principles were hammered home during employee training, a combination of role-playing and huddle sessions that emphasized and reinforced company beliefs. The objective of this "training": acquiescence and coalescence. Employees realized it was the company's way or the highway. Every employee needed to think alike. Those who failed to comply or be unified did not last long. Play along and your job was safe.

The firm's senior executives believed devotion to its tenets eliminated complexity. Counterintuitive thinking, alternative views and approaches, exceptions to the rule, and personal perspectives and opinions all limited productivity. The executives were of the opinion that contrary thoughts birthed incurable maladies, infections that should be eradicated immediately. More specifically, the person spreading the ailment should be dismissed before his or her dangerous thoughts infected the entire workforce.

For the "system" to function optimally and for revenue targets to be met, everyone had to stick to the program, working in a regimented fashion. Thus, the company language was standardized to ensure all associates conveyed a consistent message to the market. The "script" included reasons why the customer would be wise to work with them and fools to work with their competitors. Management valued how its process simplified staff oversight. The more alike people were, the easier they were to manage. Their approach left little room for individuality. Dissenters were labeled a distraction, destined to depart the firm.

Simon knew it was par for the course for a corporation like Unlimited Resources to function in this manner. Their operations were global, with offices scattered across the United States, China, India, Europe, South America, and other emerging markets. Success in one territory fueled expansion into another. The company's motto was "Nothing succeeds better than success." To management, enlarging one's market share was not only justified but inevitable. Simon called it "Corporate Manifest Destiny," a God-given right to expand one's business, and a credo that every manager at the firm had to subscribe to. As they were told on a daily basis, "Stagnation is the prelude to elimination, and the antidote to stagnation is more market share."

Simon understood corporate America functioned from a different set of principles than his own. That never bothered him. He recognized—even appreciated—the importance of free markets, profit motives, and Adam Smith's "invisible hand" being a guiding force in a healthy economic system. But he couldn't help noticing how companies manipulated that hand toward its own ends.

Simon believed people are shepherded by self-interest. He saw too many signs of how innately selfish humans could be. Every now and then they may function altruistically, allowing their more enlightened selves to dictate their actions. Corporations, on the other hand, seem always to be steered by its main interest: profit. Rightfully so, Simon thought.

Attention to the top and bottom line is paramount. The machine requires continual lubrication, without which those revenue goals will not be met. And while from time to time companies seize opportunities to be compassionate and considerate toward others, an agenda may lie behind it: some tax break or governmental incentive that bolsters the bottom line. At best, their motives are questionable. Down the road, "downsizing" may be the course of action that offsets their generous contribution and shores up the profit-and-loss column.

Simon felt working for his last employer had robbed him of something intangible, pushing his cherished memories further into the distance and challenging his ability to retrieve and draw strength from them. For that company, *doing* would always be more important than *being*. He often wondered why employers felt the need to corral its resources, establishing boundary lines to fence them in. He preferred staff to be unleashed, allowing them to be themselves, harnessing their individual abilities toward some united goal. He saw their individuality as an asset opposed to a deficit.

Rigid approaches choke creativity and turn a blind eye toward alternate routes to success. For Simon, the company he was about to start would be the proving ground for his theories and beliefs.

Ping. Looking up, he realized they had reached the tenth floor.

The cube-like box continued its upward journey and another wave of introspection overtook him.

He thought about Ray, a friend of his dad, who gave him his first "real" job. Until then it had been childhood entrepreneurial ventures: a paper route (Simon smiles when he thinks about going door to door to collect payment for the weekly distribution), shoveling driveways in the winter, mowing lawns in the summer, and a part-time job at a local pizzeria.

Ray was a good-natured professional who always emphasized the importance of family, relationships, and hard work. When he hired someone, he gave the same speech: "We are hiring *you,* so be *you.* Some days you will like what you are doing; other days you won't. Regardless, work your ass off. In time, you'll be recognized. You're not the only amazing person who has been hired by this company. Make time to get to know your fellow employees. At the end of the day, go home and be kind to your family and friends. Good relationships make full lives. Come back tomorrow, punch in your timecard, and do it again."

Ping. Simon looked up. They had reached the fourteenth floor. He noticed everyone still resisting the urge to gaze at other passengers. Soon enough they would egress from the metal box and be thrust into a whirlwind of calls, pipeline meetings, and business dealings requiring their full attention. The day's demands necessitated uncompromising focus.

With no one to engage in conversation, Simon resumed staring at the floor.

Then a jerking motion arrested everyone's attention. The elevator stalled between floor fifteen and sixteen.

One of the passengers spoke the obvious: "We're stuck!"

Simon chuckled. He loved a clear case of double entendre. *These passengers have no idea how "stuck" they are,* he thought.

He started to think about Michael with whom he had worked at Unlimited Resources. Michael hated working there but decided one reason to stay outweighed numerous reasons to leave: Money. Moola. Greenbacks. Dinero. The Big Bucks. The Almighty Dollar.

Before joining the company, Michael negotiated a fantastic base salary, which, combined with their bonus program and the restricted stock units they awarded, left him chained to the job until he could cash in on those benefits. Vesting schedules have a funny way of doing that. His had predetermined sale dates that wouldn't allow him to take full advantage until years of indentured service had elapsed, unless of course he chose to walk away, leaving money on the table. But he found it difficult to free himself from the proverbial "golden handcuffs."

The hope of a big payout instilled in him an extreme level of tolerance, helping him overlook the irksome, tedious day-to-day hassles imposed by management's style. Attending weekly sales meetings, fielding endless questions from management about his sales activity, taking orders from clients, developing business prospects, presenting options to the client, and finally closing deals—all of it had a redundant nature that would have tried the patience of Job. But with family obligations, a modest amount of debt, and a lifestyle standard to uphold, it made sense for Michael to stay put. Any levelheaded person would grant these were reasonable justifications.

Nevertheless, if Michael were asked while sitting at a bar as he sipped Macallan 18, he would admit he felt trapped. Earlier in his career, he'd dreamed of starting his own firm but as each year passed, that dream receded into the background. The tyranny of today with its fresh set of demands bullied him into forgetting his aspiration, one which still lay dormant in his heart.

Objectively speaking, though, Michael was carving out a

nice career. He earned great money and had created a nice life for himself and his family: the kids went to private schools, he drove a Porsche 911, and bonuses covered the vacations he and his family embarked on each year, visiting distant lands on their bucket list.

Having developed a close friendship with him, Simon knew this image of a happy life belied Michael's true feelings. Michael chose enchanting stability over the less defined, albeit seductive, entrepreneurial opportunity he dreamed of. He stayed put and rested on the security of nominal annual increases, meager bonuses, and managers' respect for his consistent revenue generation.

Michael knew he should have left long ago, but he became complacent. The mechanical nature of the operation, with its soulless pursuit of profit and gouging of clients to achieve mandated gross margins, troubled his simpler business sensibilities, but he never made a move to change his situation. He never mustered up the courage to part ways with the company and opted not to venture down an unknown road in an attempt to forge something out of nothing.

Simon left Unlimited Resources, and Michael continued to toil away like Bob Cratchit, Dickens's abused and underpaid accounting clerk in *A Christmas Carol*. Management continued to take advantage of Michael but he tolerated it.

A jolt rocked the elevator, and it resumed its ascent. The light for the seventeenth floor shone but went unnoticed by all but Simon. His heart began to race. One more floor and he would exit and commence a new phase in his career, one he hoped would be marked by—

Ping. The human boxcar had finally reached its destination.

The doors retracted into their respective slots, and the others walked out militaristically, turning left. The doors to Unlimited Resources automatically opened, and one by one all filed in. A labyrinth of cubicles could be seen from the lobby. Simon's elevator "companions" dispersed and moved like mice hunting for a nob of cheese in a maze.

A sympathetic familiarity made Simon contemplative. He knew that environment all too well. For five years he had turned left upon reaching the eighteenth floor.

Today he would turn right.

Before heading into the office space for the new company he'd recently founded, he paused and took a moment to reflect. He recalled how he had vacillated for years between should and shouldn't, could and couldn't, do and don't. Then he finally made the choice to leave his old employer; he had crossed his personal Rubicon. Now, standing on the shoreline of his new venture, the following raced through his mind:

Endings somewhere become beginnings elsewhere. One's journey is a spectrum of movements, each step part of a continuum. My "here" is connected to "there." Every step taken has impacted who I am today. The road changes and eventually changes you. Established patterns and old logic must be transcended. Better to face the howling unknown of the sea than the familiar comfort of the shore. Challenging paths lead to heights of greatness.

Simon turned right. In bold red lettering a small placard contained the word *DIVERSUM*. He decided on that name for his company because it means "different" in Latin. Underneath it he added a tagline: "Where working for me means I'm working for you."

He opened the door, swinging it until it clicked in place against a circular magnet attached to the wall. He turned and stared across the foyer, looking at the entrance to his former employer. Their office bustled with enthusiasm; his radiated silence. The difference between his singular portal and their grand entryway accentuated the options awaiting those exiting the elevator on the eighteenth floor.

Simon knew the gravitational pull his old firm possessed, with its well-established reputation in the marketplace. It definitely had an appeal, but he hoped there were those seeking something different, something less impersonal, something that valued men and women over the machine.

SPARK PLUGS

- The "machine" is a metaphor for an impersonal workplace that has a negative impact on its employees. What are some words or metaphors you would use to describe your work environment?
- In what ways does the company you work for promote being unique? Or do you think it fosters homogeneity? On one side of a note card list ways companies can promote individuality, and on the other side list ways it can stifle it.
- List five words that define who you are, and then ask yourself if your job allows you to be yourself.
- Accept the following: corporate America functions from a set of principles based on making a profit. Look up the word *capitalism* and write its definition on one side of a note card. On the other side, list three pros and three cons of the concept of capitalism.
- Some corporations standardize and homogenize everything, including its employees, leaving no room for individualism. Would that business model work for you as an employer? Why or why not?
- The best employers are those who appreciate and value the gifts and talents their employees possess. If

you can't be yourself in your job, it may not be the right job for you.

- Counterintuitive thinking, alternative views and approaches, and unorthodox values are good traits to have even if a company does not value them.

PART 2

MAINTENANCE TIPS FOR OPTIMUM CAREER PERFORMANCE

3 TAKE OWNERSHIP OF YOUR CAREER

IF THE STORIES IN CHAPTERS 1 AND 2—ABOUT MICE meandering through mazes and Simon ascending the elevator to his new company—were meant to teach you anything, it is that you must take your career into your own hands. Left to your employer, its trajectory will follow a predetermined path comprised of annual reviews that may or may not lead to changes in salary, position, and title—a slow ascent, if at all, up the proverbial corporate ladder.

Surely there must be a better way to build a career of distinction and achieve one's career goals. There is. But not everyone is willing to do what it takes.

The reality is this: when it comes to their careers, most are complacent about them or satisfied with others managing them. They are content to follow a fanciful "yellow brick road," hoping they reach Emerald City, the place where they think their "dream job" awaits. They reason with themselves, *Why stress and strive to find and fulfill my calling when someone else can do it for me?* But reliance on another person in this regard is an unwise strategy.

And pocket-sized aspirations and anemic ambitions are minimal help—they will only take you so far. Sadly, many are okay with that. They find comfort in the status quo—standing out is unimportant to them. They prefer to avoid the solitary journey of the "career hero" who pursues his or her calling at all costs. That path, they determine, is far too arduous. Or maybe they just do not know how to improve their corporate lot in life.

For your work life to improve and for your career to be all you want it to be—if you want its engine to rev and hum—you must take ownership of it. It is the first order of business in tuning up your career. You cannot rely on others to determine its outcome or what it should be. Parents, partners, or any other significant people in your life are not obligated to make *your* career happen for you. Neither is your employer obliged to help develop it for you, even though some companies create career tracks for their staff.

A career engine never runs right if the individual has not taken full responsibility for it. Accepting responsibility for your life of employment does two things. First, it gives you control. You become the master of your destiny. You direct the course of your future, independent of the desires, expectations, and machinations of others. (I am a bit reluctant to use the phrase "master of your destiny" because no one is ever in complete control. So much in our lives is outside our ability to direct and influence, such as other people's behavior or certain events that happen around us. Only the egomaniacal think they are in total control.) Secondly, accepting responsibility for your work life removes all excuse-making options and finger pointing—a tough pill for some to swallow since it means everything stands or falls with them. Control and responsibility are two sides of the same coin.

Most people like the idea of having control but not so much the aspect of taking responsibility for their decisions and actions.

They prefer to retain the right to blame someone or something if things don't turn out as they had hoped. But truly owning your career means you are left only with yourself to applaud or accuse. Maybe that's why most employees leave career decisions to their employers: the onus of success or failure is too much to bear. The bottom line: personal accountability is the foundation of every noteworthy career.

Often I turn to myths to help me better understand concepts like fate, hubris, heroism, justice, beauty, and even personal accountability. More than mere stories, myths are sacred tales that explain the world and the experience of being human. They help us posture ourselves for proper action. One in particular, the myth of Orestes, is quite instructive when it comes to the matter of "owning up" and taking responsibility.

Orestes was the grandson of Atreus, who in his arrogance tried to prove himself stronger than the gods. As a result, the gods punished him and cursed his descendants, including Clytemnestra, Orestes's mother. The enactment of this curse included Clytemnestra killing her husband, Orestes's father.

This created a dilemma for Orestes: he had to honor a Greek code that required him to kill the person who murdered his father, *but* the greatest sin a Greek could commit was the sin of matricide, killing one's mother. To meet the expectations of the code, he would need to murder his mother, which would then destine him to live a cursed life.

Orestes agonized over his dilemma but still decided to do what had to be done and killed his mother. The gods then punished him for this sin and sent the Furies—creatures with the head and body of a woman and a bird's wings and talons—to torment him.

After years of reflection and self-loathing, Orestes petitioned the gods to remove the curse. The gods hold a trial, at which Apollo, Olympian god of the sun, light, music, and everything beautiful, defended Orestes and let the tribunal know he himself had orchestrated the whole situation and thus Orestes should not be held liable—he had had no choice but to kill his mother.

Despite Apollo's confession and ardent plea, Orestes told the gods he was still responsible for all that had happened. The crummy hand he had been dealt was the result of his choices. The gods, shocked because they had never seen anyone take total responsibility for their actions, relented and reversed the curse, and the Furies were transformed into Eumenides, benign spirits who sent good fortune to Orestes.

Orestes did not ask, "How in the world did I end up here?" He did not whine, "Why did this happen to me?" He neither carped about nor criticized the actions of others. Nowhere in the story does he blame his family, even though his grandfather's actions caused his life to be cursed, and neither did he accuse the gods or "fate" for the terrible torments that came his way, even though Apollo admitted he'd had a hand in his misfortune. Instead, he accepted his reality, petitioned for help, and sought a solution to what most would call a shitty situation.

There will always be ample opportunities to find fault with others and plenty of reasons to "curse the gods" for the troubles, hardships, and obstacles you encounter on your career path: those who do not value your contribution to the organization, mean-hearted managers who denigrate your performance, back-stabbing coworkers, a corporate transaction that moves your job overseas, or an acquisition that eliminates your job. You can add to this list daily: most workdays bring a reason or two as to why you should feel upset and why you are not "getting your due."

You may have heard some of the excuses used by others in relation to their vocational shortfalls:

- "I can't catch a break. Nothing ever goes my way. It's like a black cloud is hanging over my head."

- "I have limited connections, limited education, and limited talent."
- "I am too young and lack experience." (Later these turn into "I'm too old and have too much experience.")
- "I'll never make it. I'm destined to fail." (The epitome of negative self-talk.)
- "My employer doesn't value me."
- "Some have all the luck. Not me."
- "I got 'downsized' . . . again."

The story of Orestes recommends this: reject excuse-making and refuse participation in the blame game. Pointing the finger at people and problems prevents progress. It pushes the pause button on reaching your potential and puts off for another day what you are meant to accomplish today.

You cannot dodge accountability and still expect to advance toward the career you want.

Sometimes organizations limit your professional growth and/or earning potential. There are times you reach a point where you have maxed out your upside at a company. So what do you do when you feel someone else is in control of your career and the money associated with it? Said another way, what do you do when you feel the rewards at work are not commensurate with your efforts? (Truth be told, we are all on the hunt for as much "cheese" as we can find—everyone wants to be rewarded as much as possible for their efforts.)

A friend of mine had a good run with his employer; he lived at the top of the sales scorecard five years straight. There was never a reporting cycle where his revenue production dipped below what it was the quarter before. The money he generated for the company rose quarter after quarter, year after year. Five. Years. Straight. Impressive! He made them millions.

Strangely, around the fourth year of his employment with them, his bonuses began to drop. Confused, he inquired why this was so. Management responded with the following: "There are more mouths to feed." He was told the bonus pool needed to be equally shared among the salesforce, including the employees recently added to the team. The compensation policy specified that the money allocated for bonuses get divvied up evenly among the team members, regardless of one's tenure or individual performance. In actuality, 75 percent was divided evenly, and the remaining 25 percent was allocated based on "managerial discretion."

While he hoped his positive year-over-year performance would translate into more personal earnings, it never did. Management expected he would be content with his portion of the bonus dollars along with the stock he was awarded when the company became publicly traded: he was not.

In private, he discussed the matter with his supervisor and asked what more he could do to ensure a bigger piece of the pie. Her response left him befuddled. "Nothing more could be done," she said. "The bonus policy is what it is." My friend realized there was no longer any upside potential. Whether he generated more or less revenue, his bonuses were calculated according to the compensation model used by management. He could only hope that a portion of the "managerial discretion" money made its way into his pocket.

So, he had a decision to make: stay and accept a level of dissatisfaction every time bonuses were distributed, or leave and find an employer that better incentivized their employees. He left. And then started his own business so he could exercise control over how rewards were doled out to himself and others.

Dissatisfaction at a job happens often, and sometimes unforeseen events turn your work world upside down. Just look at Steve Jobs's story. On September 16, 1985, he was forced out of Apple, the company he founded. Different factors contributed to the event: a woefully slow computer, problems with its internal hard disk drive, declining sales, and losing a boardroom battle with then CEO, John Sculley, whom Jobs had hired. Jobs had no choice but to accept the decision of the board of directors. Whether he agreed or not, he had to "own it" when it came to Apple's initial failures.[1]

But Jobs wrested his career out of the clutch of failure and took matters into his own hands. The situation prompted him to reimagine his career: he started a new company called NeXT, which he later sold to Apple for $400 million. Before long, Jobs would become Apple's CEO. As with Orestes, the "curses" he experienced turned into "blessings" *after* he accepted responsibility for what had happened in the earlier stages of Apple's evolution.

You will never have the career you want if others dictate what it should be and set its parameters for you. The influence and input of others is invaluable; career accomplishments are seldom, if ever, solo efforts. But complete reliance on others to make it happen for you is another thing altogether and should be rejected.

At this point in your career, you may feel like you are "going through the paces"; you have religiously followed the career development program your employer has had for you. And there is nothing wrong with that. But now you are ready for your career to be one of distinction, one in which you exercise greater control. You feel your job should be more meaningful than it is, and you want to have a stronger hand in determining its outcome: you want to remove the gunk preventing peak performance.

Maybe others have thwarted your progress. Maybe unexpected events at the company you work or worked for have derailed you and impeded your career advancement. What should you do? What will you do?

Ask yourself, *Has my career engine begun to sputter? Has it seized up?* If so, it's time to tune it up before it stops completely. The best thing you can do at this juncture is this: accept full responsibility for all that has happened up to this point, flush out any excuses you have been making, and quit blaming those who may have hindered your progress. Then determine what you want to happen next.

SPARK PLUGS

- One way to get where you are going career-wise is to follow the career track your employer has for you. Better still is taking ownership of what you do for a living—don't pawn off the responsibility of your life's work on someone else.

- Take some time to think about what you really want to do career-wise. Are you working toward that end? Do you wish you were in a different role or wish you were doing something totally different? Map out five action steps to get where you want to be.

- Taking ownership of your career puts you in control of its destiny, but it also removes all excuses for how it turns out. You are left with only yourself to applaud and accuse.

- Have you been making excuses as to why your career is not all you hoped it would be? List on a note card your three most common excuses.

- On the other side of that note card, write the ways you can turn those excuses into actions that change your circumstances (i.e., instead of bitching about your current employer's commission plan, find a job that offers a better compensation model).

- Remember: personal accountability is the foundation of every noteworthy career.
- Re-read the myth of Orestes. Note how the Furies were turned into Eumenides. List any negatives in your life that can be turned into positives by taking responsibility for your career and life.

4 DON'T LOOK NOW, BUT YOU MAY BE AN ENTREPRENEUR

ONE WAY YOU CAN TAKE TOTAL CONTROL OF YOUR CAREER is by becoming an entrepreneur. A fine-sounding notion. A grand idea. But a road not easily traveled. Entrepreneurship is not as easy as you may think.

The story of every successful entrepreneur includes the following: challenges, struggles, obstacles, and difficulties that needed to be worked through, overcome, solved, and sometimes ignored. That said, this type of "tune-up" can lead to an exhilarating, life-altering, self-gratifying experience. Entrepreneurship is career ownership at its highest level. Like the old Esso (now ExxonMobil) slogan used to state, it's like putting "a tiger in your [career] tank."

Most people color inside the lines; some do not. There are those who think and act in accordance with set rules; they are conventional and orthodox in outlook and approach. Others see alternatives, an array of possibilities as to how things can be done— in either a better or a different way.

Does something about this resonate with you? Do you look at the success of others and ask, *If they can do it, why can't I?*

When you look at others, does their work life seem inconsequential, indistinct, and unambitious compared to what you desire for your own career? Are you a frustrated "jack-in-the-box" because you constantly think "outside the box"?

Much has been written about successful entrepreneurs: what traits they possess, how they made their fortunes, what you need to do to be like them, and more. Having read a wide range of material on such success stories, including the likes of Henry Ford, Estée Lauder, Steve Jobs, Stan Lee, Bobby Flay, P.T. Barnum, Indra Nooyi, Richard Branson, Sam Walton, Joyce C. Hall, and other lesser known entrepreneurs like Igor Sikorsky, Whitney Wolfe Herd, Victor Kiam, Wang Yung-ching, Scott Lee, Peter X. Kelly, and Anthony Trama, the following seems to be the most common features among them all, well-known or not:

- They were willing to start from scratch: it did not matter if the person had means or not.
- They worked with what they had and understood the bottom is as good a starting place as any.
- The beginning stages of their companies were humble; the founders were *not* overnight successes. Rather, they toiled and labored in anonymity—in basements, garages, and small apartments—before ever becoming known for what made them famous. Starting small was not a problem to them; thinking small was.
- Failure pockmarked their experience: many tried other ventures and were unsuccessful. Yet they kept at it and believed as Theodore Roosevelt did when he said, "Far better it is to dare mighty things, to win glorious triumphs, *even though checkered by failure* . . . than to rank with those poor spirits who neither

enjoy nor suffer much, because they live in a gray twilight that knows not victory nor defeat" (italics mine).

- Some held other jobs while they worked on their "dream." Henry Ford is a classic case: he continued to work at Thomas Edison's Illuminating Company while he pursued his "gas-engine experiments." Others cleaned offices, dug ditches, performed clerical work, and served as dishwashers and busboys while attending to their "dream job" after hours.

- Their road to success was *not* a direct route: they reached their destinations after traveling winding paths. It is not atypical for an entrepreneur to head in one direction only to be redirected elsewhere. Steps and missteps are all part of the journey, and it often takes both to get from point A to point B.

- Determination is more important than degrees: Education is invaluable and can be an important contributor toward success, but minus a mindset on doggedly pursuing your goals, they will never be reached. There are plenty of success stories of people without a high school education; rare are those of people who lacked unwavering adherence to a purpose.

- Dark backdrops create a desire to break out of one's existing environment. Many entrepreneurs wanted a better life than the one they knew. Brandon Steiner, founder of Steiner Sports, jokes that he "saw the light [of entrepreneurship] at an early age—the light of an empty refrigerator."[1] Nothing puts fire in your belly more than hunger. Nothing makes you more pragmatic than life's harsher impositions. Dark days make you long for a different, more radiant reality.

Boil it all down and here is what you get: entrepreneurs are normal people who "go for it." They have no magic formula, no silver bullet. They started *somewhere* and then worked their asses off. Entrepreneurs have guts—guts to try, guts to pull out all the stops, guts to go all out, guts to put their heart and soul into *something.*

Like gutsy Matsushita Konosuke, who saw a way to improve upon an existing product. As they say, "Build a better mousetrap and the world will beat a path to your door." He built it.

He started working at the age of nine to support his family. Eventually, he landed a job at the Ōsaka Electric Light Company, where he rapidly ascended the corporate ladder, even though he lacked a formal education. While there, he came up with an idea for an improved light socket, which his unenthusiastic boss flat-out rejected. Matsushita felt compelled to leave the company to further explore his idea.

And that landed him in the basement of his tenement.

For a period of time, nothing happened. His company seemed destined for failure. He offered samples of his product to wholesalers, but they wanted more than one product from their suppliers. On the verge of bankruptcy, he received an unexpected order for insulator plates for fans, which he knew how to make. The revenue from this order allowed him to continue his work related to his light socket project. Later, when wholesalers recognized the superiority of his invention—and that it had a cheaper price tag—the orders came in. Matsushita Konosuke went on to found Panasonic.

Nothing magical. Nothing mysterious. Nothing supernatural. Just an idea, a lot of hard work, and a bit of luck.

Aviator Nation, the high-end clothing brand known for its comfortable, colorful, chill clothing, was started in a garage in Venice, California. It's founder, Paige Mycoskie, a Texas native, fell in love with the California vibe—and its picturesque views—

after she appeared on the adventure reality show *The Amazing Race*. After she walked on the beach and saw people playing volleyball, throwing frisbees, biking, and rollerblading, she dreamed up an idea for a clothing line.

But retail was not her first choice. She first pursued a career in journalism, but it left her unfulfilled. So she quit and took a job at a surf shop in Venice Beach (the first step in taking ownership of her career). After she completed her shifts, she began to design her own retro, surf-inspired clothes. Obsessed with comfort, she made it her goal to create clothes that resembled the hip, laid-back culture of the '70s—and the free and easy beach aura of Venice. Since those humble beginnings in her garage in 2006, Mycoskie's Aviator Nation has generated sales that have ranged from $70 million in 2020 to $110 million in 2021. Those numbers are projected to at least double by 2023.

Again, nothing extraordinary—no waving of a wand, no hocus pocus. Just a girl with a dream, a willingness to work her ass off to make it happen, and the determination to see it through.

Entrepreneurship is not for everyone. But maybe it is right for you. In your mind, it may be the smartest and safest way to take control of your career. If you feel you are busting at the seams at your current place of employment, if you are asking yourself, *Why I am doing all this to make* them *money when I can be making the money for myself?*, if you feel your job is keeping you from what you were intended to do, then maybe you should venture out, start your own firm, and build your own business.

If this is the path you choose to take, remember the following:

- Do not despise the days of small beginnings.
  Important work takes time to develop. Rome wasn't
  built in a day, as they say. Neither was the rebuilding

of the Temple of the Jews around 520 BC. After the fall of Jerusalem, the Israelites lived as exiles in Babylon. Before any of this happened, however, prophets like Ezekiel and Jeremiah promised that God would one day restore the nation of Israel to their homeland. Part of that restoration included rebuilding the temple, which lay in ruins. Discouraged by the ruinous site, the prophet Zechariah prodded the people with this challenge: "Who dares despise the day of small things . . . ?" (Zechariah 4:10). The reality: grand undertakings often appear insignificant at first. Countless business successes have sprung from humble origins. Remember: starting small is never wrong, but thinking small always is.

- Accept failure as part of the process. Here is where everyone references the failures and setbacks experienced by Abraham Lincoln before he was elected president of the United States. Noted. Instead, let's consider Joe Torre, baseball player, coach, and MLB executive. His career as a coach was not particularly awe-inspiring . . . at first. Here's what his first fourteen years looked like: a .405 winning percentage as coach for the New York Mets over a five-year span, a .529 win percentage over three years with the Atlanta Braves, and a .498 win percentage with the St. Louis Cardinals over six years —an overall average below .500 percent. And it should be noted he was fired from all three teams. It was not until he coached the New York Yankees that he experienced what most baseball aficionados would call coaching success, achieving a win percentage of

.605 over a twelve-year span and winning six pennants and four World Series titles.

- Wait for the right moment. Most entrepreneurs are eager, not impetuous. While there are plenty of successful "movers and shakers" who fire before they aim, having a plan never hurt anyone. In other words, think through your moves. Maybe save up some seed money for your new venture before quitting your job. Maybe work into the wee hours of the morning on your dream job while still employed elsewhere. Maybe consult with friends and family before embarking on vast ventures. Then again, sometimes the right moment means leaving it all behind and going for it. As Tess Vigeland says in her book *Leap*, there are times you feel compelled to hand in your "workplace divorce papers."[2] Only you can decide.

- Use your intuition. In an essay entitled "A Mysterious Faculty," Igor Sikorsky bats around the idea of intuition—what some might call thinking outside the box—and its relation to success. After admitting that the true nature of intuition cannot be understood, he concludes it is "an extremely primitive . . . faculty of higher order."[3] Thomas Edison and Henry Ford succeeded, he says, because their intuition allowed them to *envision* the future and then "direct their efforts accordingly."[4] Edison admitted as much, saying he received "impressions" from the universe that had to be worked out. Another way to say all this is to say sometimes you just have to "go with your gut."

Nothing gets your career engine going like being an

entrepreneur. But entrepreneurship is not for everyone. It is a road less traveled but one worth traveling if you determine it is the only way you can live out your career as you've always wanted.

SPARK PLUGS

- The best way to take control of your career may be by becoming an entrepreneur, but being one is not for everyone. Think twice (at least) before committing to that course.
- Have you thought about ways to make a product better or how to improve upon a business service? Do you ask yourself, *If they can do it, why can't I?* Do you have an idea for something no one else has made or done? If you answer these questions in the affirmative, you may be a candidate for entrepreneurship.
- Think about an entrepreneur you admire and compare the traits that made them successful to those listed in this chapter. Ask yourself what traits people would use to describe you.
- On the front of a note card, list five or more pros of being an entrepreneur, and on the back, list any cons you can think of.
- My definition of an *entrepreneur* is an average person who "goes for it." How would you define *entrepreneur?*
- If you could start your own business, what would it be? Create a step-by-step action plan for it. Have some fun with this exercise and start by thinking of different names for your company.

5 WRONG MOVES ARE NOT FINAL MOVES

You may have concluded, based on the reasons noted in the last chapter, that you are meant to be an entrepreneur—you have an idea for something no one else has thought of or made, or you've come up with a design for a better mousetrap, or maybe deep down you know you can provide the same service as someone else, only better. There is certainly no better way for a career engine to be at full throttle.

But . . . you still work for someone else.

It could be you missed an opportunity to branch off on your own. Maybe you've been pursuing the career that your parents wanted for you or one you thought you wanted but don't want anymore. Do you look back at the steps you have taken and wish you could erase them all, choose a different path, and start over again?

It sounds a bit mystical, but all steps taken on a career journey are interconnected. They are on a continuum: last steps on one road are connected to the first steps on another; ground already traversed leads to the new ground you are about to travel. In other words, every step—and misstep—has led you to the very place you now find yourself. Any "wrong" moves you think you've made are not final moves.

If you have worked ten years or more, you have made some "wrong" moves. Worry not. You are in good company. Everyone has stumbled, slipped, or tripped as they have traveled down their career path. But maybe your missteps were not wrong at all. Maybe you headed in one direction only for it to lead to another road you were meant to explore. For the sake of argument, let's agree a "wrong" move does not preclude you from making another move.

A necessary part of the mental "maintenance" to be performed on your career is to realize careers are complex, a word defined in nuanced fashion by *Webster's New Universal Unabridged Dictionary*. The definition of the word *complex* is derived from Latin and means "to weave and to braid." In other words, that which is complex consists of interlaced strands that form a more intricate pattern, like a stylish hair braid or boat rope.

Your career is made of different "strands" woven together. Frankenstein-like, most careers are stitched jointly with various parts to form something greater—and stronger—than each part can be separately. They are a cluster of distinctive characteristics that include right and wrong moves, steps and missteps, ground gained and sometimes lost.

It is not uncommon to pursue one vocation only to scrap it for something else. Not everyone knows from an early age what they are meant to be or do for a living for the rest of their life. Most fumble about until they discover it, as if by chance. Consider these examples of those who *eventually* found what they were looking for:

Best known for his Orin Swift and The Prisoner wine labels, Dave Phinney achieved success by disrupting a profession known for its zealots of tradition. While the old guard preferred not to mess with traditional wine-making formulas, Phinney wanted to produce affordable outstanding wines while removing industry snobbery in the process—and he wanted to accomplish both by crafting a "blend." What most do not know: Phinney studied political science and pursued a career as a public defender. After a change of heart, he changed direction and ended up a vintner.

Arlete Turturro dreamed of opening a children's clothing store on Madison Avenue and attended the Fashion Institute of Technology to work toward that end. She interned at B. Altman and Company and quickly became the company's youngest buyer ever. But marriage and children altered her plans. When she reentered the workforce, she opted not to go into fashion retail and obtained a real estate license and worked for a real estate development company. Part of her job was to hire cleaning crews for the office buildings the company managed. She recognized the cleaning business had a low barrier of entry and required little capital to start. She tapped her network—the clients she managed—and asked if they would allow her to clean the offices they occupied. What started as a one-person side gig turned into a thirty-employee company.

Jorge Mario Bergoglio served as a janitor during the day and a bouncer in the evening. He also trained to be a chemist and worked as a technician in a food service laboratory. He felt unfulfilled with all these endeavors, so he joined the Jesuits and went on to be ordained as a Catholic priest. In 2013 Bergoglio became Pope Francis and was ratified as the head of the Catholic Church and sovereign of the Vatican City.

Tom Monaghan was placed in a Catholic orphanage at an early age. Later he attended seminary with plans to be a priest but was expelled for a series of disciplinary infractions. A stint in the marines followed but ended with him being discharged. He and his brother then borrowed money to buy a pizza store named DomiNick's. Later he changed the name to Domino's. After he dropped sub sandwiches from the menu and began focusing on delivery to college campuses, the pizza chain took off. (He even invented a new insulated box for the pizzas, which allowed him to stack them and deliver more than one pie at a time.) At the end of 2021, company revenues totaled $4.36 billion, and as of 2022, there are 18,848 locations, with new franchises being added daily.

Harvey Firestone started as a traveling medicine-extract salesman and then founded the Firestone Tire and Rubber Company. J. C. Penney started as a butcher and then established a major retail enterprise. Caryn Elaine Johnson, aka Whoopi Goldberg, was a waitress, bank teller, mortuary cosmetologist— even a bricklayer—before her career in Hollywood. The list goes on.

What is common among them: each headed in one direction and then, for whatever reason, charted a new course.

Each took their career into their own hands and now serves as a reminder that a change in direction—making a "right" move *after* a "wrong" one—might be the best decision you ever make. All that matters is your response to the self-perceived "wrong move." As Stephen R. Covey says in his book *The 7 Habits of Highly Effective People*, "Our response to any *mistake* affects the quality of the next moment" (italics mine).[1] In other words, do not let your next career move be governed by the moves already made, whether you think they were right or wrong or if they moved you forward or backward.

You must remain open to new directions and never allow yourself to be a prisoner of your own vocational biases. What you deem an innocuous inclination or passive prejudice toward one career track may prevent you from migrating toward what you are actually meant to do for a living. Sometimes an interesting development or an unexpected moment precedes what you were destined for. It is possible to plan on one future and end up with a totally different existence. Do not be so wedded to your preconceived notions about your career that you fail to see the golden opportunity right before your eyes.

Allow me to use my own career as an example.

My college and postgraduate years—about nine in total—were spent in preparation for the ministry. My singular focus was a life of service to God: theological studies, learning to read and write biblical Greek, serving as youth minister and worship leader, and leading Bible studies—all of which culminated in a pastorate. My career in the ministry was well under way. Some would say it was set in stone.

Then, for personal reasons, I laid aside these aspirations and plans. Immature and feeling a bit lost, I wondered who would hire someone whose training and skills were geared toward pastoral ministry. Luckily, my dad had a connection at Security Pacific Bank who offered me my first postministry job. A few years later I met Michelle Patterson, a market leader for one of the largest staffing firms in the United States. She believed the skills I had cultivated for the ministry translated well into a business development role within the staffing industry. My encounter with her set the stage for all I would go on to accomplish.

After a few years working for Security Pacific, the division I worked in was acquired by another bank, and my position was relocated to Minnesota. Opposed to relocating to the land of ten thousand Lakes, I sought employment elsewhere and interviewed with Michelle. She persuaded me that working for Robert Half International afforded me a different kind of "message" to "preach" but one that still allowed me to influence people, which, in her quick analysis of me during my interview, seemed important to me. Her assessment was correct. So, over the span of a few years, I transitioned from pastor to banker to business development professional in the staffing industry, a quizzical transformation with interesting career developments, to say the least.

How does someone with a master of arts in theological studies end up finding jobs for certified public accountants?

The answer: adaptation. Circumstances changed, and I adapted.

You will find over the course of your career, circumstances will change, whether they originate at home or at the office or in the world at large. That is a reality you must accept. How you adapt and the decisions you make that affect the "quality of the next moment," as Covey says, are all that matters. That's how I went from providing spiritual guidance to offering career guidance: by being willing to shift and making a slight change in direction. "Sometimes all it takes for us to find the meaning in what we're doing," says Tess Vigeland, "is just to have that *shift* in our perspective" (italics mine).[2] Sadly, many careers are "stuck" due to an unwillingness to reposition or deviate from an original course.

Look at it this way. Servicing your career, like your car, can be a *major* or *minor* event.

Basic service checks include simple inspections, such as checking tire pressure and lubricant levels and examining filters and fan belts. Most people bring their car to the shop every three to five thousand miles for this to be done.

Likewise, your career may only need little tweaks or adjustments for it to run right. Maybe what is required is a *minor* variation off the career theme you have been exploring, a shift that better aligns your career vehicle.

Shifting allows you to adapt and refine or redefine your vocational goals. On the surface, my transition from ministry to business development in the staffing industry seems a drastic change because of the sector change I made. But in reality a common thread existed between my aspiration to pastor a church and finding jobs for others: helping people. It was a minor shift that changed the platform I used to help people.

Every three to five years an employee needs to check his or her vehicle into the "shop" for basic maintenance. These regular service checks ensure your career engine is functioning optimally and make you aware of any minor corrections that may be needed.

Other times, however, a *major* overhaul needs to happen—the engine needs to be replaced.

In terms of a career, it may look like this: You have been an accountant for ten years and just now realize you want to be a marriage and family therapist. Or you thought you wanted to be a doctor, but in actuality you would love to be a sixth grade teacher. Or you don't want to be a plumber but instead want to build houses. Or you imagined being a performer on Broadway, but deep down you have always known you want to write plays for others to perform.

You get the picture. Something is amiss, and major repair work needs to be done.

What type of service your career needs—be that minor or major—can only be determined by you.

Here are some questions to help you figure out what type of maintenance is needed:

- Does your job offer you a sense of purpose? Asked another way, is your work meaningful? What would make it more purposeful?
- Do you feel compelled to pursue another career? Are there opportunities you missed that you'd still like to explore?
- Do you find it hard to go to work because you're not a fan of the company you work for? Do your values

align with the values of the organization with whom you are employed?

- Do you feel valued by your employer? Does your employer recognize your unique contributions to the organization?
- Is your compensation commensurate with your contributions and experience?
- In general, are you happy with your job? Are you overdue to have a conversation with your supervisor about your career goals?
- Do you want to venture out on your own but are afraid to do so? What if you had a plan or created an exit strategy to make that happen?
- Are changes taking place where you work? Have those changes created new possibilities for you within the company? Have those changes given you the reasons you need to explore opportunities outside the company?

No matter what type of service your career may need, it makes no sense to stay stalled in your "nine-to-five" because you believe certain missteps have predetermined your course. Wrong moves are far from final moves and may not have been "wrong" at all. The last step on one road is connected to the first step on another, and it's never too late to take that first new step.

SPARK PLUGS

- Do you look back on your career and wish you could get a do-over? Do you think you have made some wrong moves? If so, list on a note card what you could or should have done differently.

- Name three people whose careers you admire. Find out how they got to where they are today. What common traits exist between them?
- Remember: a *wrong* move is not a *final* move; last steps on one road are connected to the first steps on another.
- Think about the complex nature of your career, the *strands* that have contributed to what it is today. List on a note card the steps and missteps that have added to the complexity of your career so far.
- Do you want to make changes to your career? What steps could you take to do so? What slight changes could you make?
- Write a paragraph about what your dream job would look like.

6 THE TEA LEAVES IN THE BOTTOM OF THE CUP

Mechanics will tell you there are at least five signs of engine failure: a knocking sound, loss of power, an excessive amount of exhaust smoke, vibrations, and worsening gas mileage. But you don't need a mechanic to tell you; your engine will. You will hear it sputter, rattle, hiss, or chug.

Corrective measures for your car can be as complicated as an engine replacement or as easy as changing or adding oil. Regardless, everyone agrees: ignoring problems—the sights and sounds of engine trouble—increases the likelihood of more issues.

The same is true when it comes to your career. If you ignore changes and developments at work, macroeconomic conditions, or what your gut is telling you about the direction you should go career-wise, you may be destined for bigger problems. Suffice it to say, your career vehicle will not make it very far down the road. Your ability to read the tea leaves in the bottom of your cup—how you interpret change—is an essential part of tuning up your career.

Consider Matt Carpenter, once a Major League Baseball player with the St. Louis Cardinals and a three-time All-Star who had put together a respectable career from his debut in 2011 through 2018, when he hit thirty-six homers, a career-high, and finished ninth in National League MVP balloting.

Then something changed. From 2019 to 2020, his combined batting average dropped to .176 and he only hit seven home runs in those two years, even though he was accustomed to hitting upward of twenty-plus homers a season. Carpenter considered retirement but deep down felt he still had "more in the tank."

That led him to seek help, which started with a call to Joey Votto, another MLB player who had experienced something similar. Votto validated Carpenter's feelings and agreed he could still be a valuable contributor on a team. He felt Matt had lost his way and needed to transform himself back into the player he once was.

Carpenter then went on a cross-country journey to fix his swing. He visited a baseball performance lab in Louisiana, met with private batting instructors in California, and consulted a former teammate in Stillwater, Oklahoma. All combined, they assisted Carpenter in his efforts to remake himself . . . and his swing.

He shed old routines, adopted some unorthodox drills, and embraced data analysis as a means to assess his at-the-plate performance. The analytics revealed the following: the mechanics of his swing had broken down, or as Carpenter described it, his swing "had gotten out of sorts." The arc of his swing was visibly different.

But that was not the only problem. He also locked his front knee too early, which adversely effected how he shifted his weight from the back side to the front side. This caused the bat to drag behind, prevented him from hitting fastballs, and affected how he adjusted to breaking balls. In his article, "'Help Me Fix This': Inside Matt Carpenter's Cross-Country Quest to

Remake His Swing," Ken Rosenthal says, "It was as if he was in a baseball form of checkmate."[1] Carpenter was stuck and defeated.

After he addressed these issues and worked toward a new approach, his swing improved. Now on the New York Yankees, Carpenter has been a major contributor to their 2022 season's success. And as of August 2022, he is batting .305 with fifteen home runs.

Every employee reaches a point in their career when changes need to be made. Future vocational outcomes are often contingent on whether one chooses to make a change or not.

My career in the staffing industry found its stride in the late 1990s and early 2000s, when I worked for a subsidiary of Deloitte and Touche, one of the Big 6 accounting firms. (Once they were known as the Big 8 and eventually became the Big 4, proving that even industries must make changes.) At that time, a couple noteworthy news releases, the Enron and WorldCom scandals, had rocked the business world. Along with the executives at these companies, Arthur Andersen, a competitor of Deloitte, was held culpable in both fiascos. From that moment on, the accounting practices of companies were scrutinized with greater intensity.

In light of these events, Deloitte's management deemed it prudent to spin off its relatively new subsidiary for fear that federal regulators may perceive there to be "independence issues" between the parent company and its ancillary business. When you serve as the external auditor to a company to verify the accuracy of their financial statements, you cannot have another division within your company maintain that company's books and records. Plain and simple: the same organization cannot create the accounting statements *and* audit them. To do so is a blatant conflict of interest. Deloitte's management recognized this. In other words, they interpreted the tea leaves in the bottom of their cup and made the necessary changes to avoid regulatory repercussions.

The subordinated entity was spun off. At the same time, a decision was made by the executives of the subsidiary to take the company public, a grand undertaking but one which held the possibility of creating a modest financial windfall for those who worked there. It did not matter to those granted founders' shares that the stock they were awarded included a vesting schedule. We were thrilled to be participating in an Initial Public Offering (IPO).

Transitions like this bring change—some good, some not so good. During that period, my boss, whom I loved to work with and for, left to start his own company, a departure that triggered a host of other changes at the managerial level: a new market leader was assigned to the Los Angeles office, and another market leader was installed as regional manager, a newly formed position within the company. Management began to lay the groundwork for a formal corporate infrastructure.

Changes like this happen all the time, whether a company goes public or not, and you can usually see them a mile away. My coworkers and I were well aware of what was happening. Winds of change were in the air.

If you look back on the different events that transpired at your places of employment, you probably sensed changes were imminent too. Maybe you made decisions in relation to what you perceived; maybe you didn't.

There was, however, one change many of us at Deloitte were not prepared for: a radical difference in the company's culture. Amid all the enthusiasm about the IPO, a subtle unsettling undercurrent was gaining strength. The atmosphere within the firm—at least within the office in which I worked—had a different vibe after we became a publicly traded organization.

Prior to the IPO, an entrepreneurial spirit filled the air. That was replaced by a more structured, standardized approach to doing business. And, to boot, management wanted everyone to look and act like the Big 6. Why that was important to them confused me, since Arthur Andersen, a Big 6 accounting firm, was embroiled in a scandal that would eventually lead to its demise. That said, management determined that its employees, including the associates we placed on projects, needed to reflect a difference between us and our competitors. A dividing line was drawn: we were a "consulting" firm; they were "staffing" companies.

Any time a circle is drawn that separates people into categories and establishes parameters that include and exclude, I get nervous. Prior to going public, I never thought twice about not being a certified public accountant or not having a master of business administration degree. But now I was concerned. To dismiss people with an air of superiority because they do not check every box related to pedigree and credentials seems shortsighted; a superstar may be overlooked. I asked myself, *How long before a sales guy with a degree in theology would find himself outside the circle?*

Would it not be better to cast a wide net when fishing for employees? Does it not make more sense to widen rather than whittle down the circle?

All this to say, my "Spidey sense" started to tingle. The company's philosophical shift and new approach to business did not sit well with me. The idea of kicking some candidates to the curb because they no longer "fit the bill" bothered me. Plus, I saw little difference between consulting and staffing. Both offered human capital to get work done that needed to be done. Something just felt off. The words from Robert Iger's book *The Ride of a Lifetime*, come to mind: "If something doesn't feel right to you, it won't be right for you."[2]

It dawned on me I was no longer a suitable match there.

Shortly thereafter I would leave and partner up with a former coworker to start our own business.

If you hope to retain control over your career, you must learn to recognize the changing landscape within the company you work for as well as the broader economic market, for it can influence the decisions a company makes that impact your employment.

Sometimes the signs are blatant, like when the chief operating officer at the bank you work for flat-out tells you the division you work in was just sold to a bank based in Minnesota; the job is still yours if you want it, only now it will be based there. Other times the signs are less obvious but still exist.

Like when a corporate coup happens.

While a coup is a sudden and violent seizure of power, visible to all at its onset, they are planned in clandestine corners, darkened halls, and shadowy corridors. They take everyone by surprise . . . except those who orchestrate them.

Such an affair happened to my business partner and me a few years after we sold our company to a national consulting firm. Unbeknownst to us, a small contingent plotted to have the chief executive officer removed from his position. Ironically, its ringleader had actually been hired a couple years prior by the CEO.

He seemed normal enough . . . at first. He supported each market and assisted any way he could to help territories grow. On the surface, he appeared to be someone you could count on if you encountered challenges or had ideas on how to expand business. There was no way of knowing he had ulterior motives. Only in looking back could we see he waited for the opportune moment to spring his trap. The devil likes to hide behind a cross.

Everyone was clueless except those in his inner circle. They knew the score.

He had garnered enough support from a few people in leadership to help him sway the thoughts of the executives at the private equity firm that backed the company. Soon thereafter, the chief executive officer was ousted, and the chief operating officer who had formed the coup slithered into his spot.

When you are part of "the rank and file," not much can be done in scenarios like this. Boardroom decisions are made, and those in the trenches are asked to soldier on; marching orders must be followed. Even though my partner and I were unhappy with what transpired, we could do nothing. We never envisioned something like *this* could happen. Our lives at work became overcast like a Jersey day before it rains. Were these dark days a sign of darker days ahead? What did they portend for us?

After the dust settled from the coup, a level of normalcy returned to our business operation. That is what happens: the big wheels of business and capitalism keep turning. Despite the craziness of what had taken place, we still had a business to run, so we got busy with what we did on a daily basis—recruiting, marketing, and closing deals.

This went on for about a year . . .

Until the self-appointed CEO started to meddle in our operation. He decided to take a more active role in the decision making related to our region. He implied things could be better, and he knew how to make it so. In essence, he wanted to change our business model from "staff-augmentation" to "consulting" (there's that word again), even though we operated at a gross margin of over 40 percent. His approach seemed foolhardy to us, but hey, he's the boss, right?

Once we carved through all the bullshit he was slinging, we realized what he really wanted was to hire one person to replace us both, someone who possessed a background in consulting and could presumably take the Southern California practice to a new level.

We were flabbergasted when, without any prior notice, we

received an email from the CEO with an attached offer letter for a candidate he wanted to hire. It was clear from reading it this person was our replacement. To add insult to injury, he asked us to extend to the candidate the offer. Pretty ballsy, huh? This sent me through the roof.

Since we knew the terms of our employment contract, we felt comfortable calling him to let him know he now had a problem in Southern California, and he best get on a plane to come speak with us face-to-face. He did . . . with the company's general counsel at his side.

The details of that meeting are unimportant. What is important is that my partner and I negotiated an exit strategy, a game plan that allowed us to retain control of our careers. Fortunately for us, we inked a deal that guaranteed our salaries would continue to be paid for eighteen months. Unfortunately for them, the Great Recession hit a week later, and the business went into the shitter.

What should you do when you catch a glimpse of impending changes at work? What should you do when the tea leaves in the bottom of your cup are telling you something? Here are a few ideas to tune up your engine, keep it humming, and help you be in the driver's seat of your own career:

- Take time to assess your progress to date. Take a hard look at how your career has evolved. Are you doing what you really want to do? Has the perceived change created an opportunity to segue into a different line of work? Is it time to start your own business? Do not make rash decisions, but ask yourself if there is an opportunity buried in the change you now face. Has it created an opening for you to revamp your vocational goals? Train yourself to interpret changes at work—and in your life—and speculate on what opportunities can come from them.

- Determine if you can live with the change. Sometimes it makes sense to go with the flow and see where it takes you. For every person who says, "This isn't going to work for me," there is someone else who is saying, "This might be good for me." Only you can say.

- If necessary, plan your exit. It may be time to look for new avenues of employment. Maybe you have maxed out your upside potential. Maybe you are no longer aligned with the organization from a philosophical standpoint. Maybe the culture within the company changed and it no longer suits you. These may be signs it is time to find a new career home. If so, avoid being impetuous but strategize about your departure.

- Expect a period of adjustment. If you stay or go, it takes time to get used to something different, like a new company, a different culture, a new boss with a different leadership style, or a new industry with different jargon. Be prepared for differences, and allow yourself the time needed to get acclimated.

Sometimes the writing on the wall is as clear as day. Other times the tea leaves are harder to comprehend. Regardless, your ability to interpret change has a direct impact on the efficacy of your career engine. The employee who ignores the sights and sounds of change will likely find himself or herself stalled.

Any change that comes your way is the perfect time for a tune-up.

SPARK PLUGS

- The ability to interpret change is essential to tuning up your career.
- Review Matt Carpenter's story again. Note his realization that something was off with his swing and his willingness to try new approaches. Think about how your career may be "off." List three ideas on how you can address any "issues" you may be facing in your career.
- Think about the changes that have transpired in your life over the last ten to fifteen years. How would you rate yourself on your ability to interpret those changes and your ability to adapt when they occurred?
- Take the following steps when you notice looming changes: consider ways the change may be creating an opportunity for you, determine if you can live with that change or not, plan your exit if you cannot live with the impending changes, and be prepared for a period of adjustment.
- Change will occur throughout your career. Those events afford you time to do a career tune-up. Take the time to consider what those changes might mean for you.

7 A STEP DOWN CAN BE A STEP UP

ONE OF THE GREATEST CAREER MISCONCEPTIONS THAT HAS befuddled employees is this: taking a step down is the worst possible thing you can do. Careers are meant to be always on the rise, most would say. And ascension up the employment ladder usually means more pay, which is a good thing, right? So why would anyone decide to head in a downward direction toward the land of indistinct titles and less pay?

God forbid you get demoted or, worse yet, you choose to demote yourself. "We assume and believe," says Tess Vigeland, "that every step on the career ladder must and will be an upward trajectory."[1] It's an inferred maxim: employees must always move *up* a career ladder, never *down*.

Stepping down in position—along with the potential salary reduction that may accompany that move—sends a signal to others, one which is open to a variety of interpretations: you are fed up with managerial bullshit, so you removed yourself from it; you are ambivalent about staying with the company and considering quitting; your job is in jeopardy; you are eyeing retirement; you are not qualified for a role at *that* level, and your boss "suggested" you step down; or you decided, for no apparent reason, to commit career suicide. It's inconceivable that such a decision might contain some wisdom or ingenuity. A choice like this violates workplace logic, doesn't it? Most think reversing course and making your way *down* rungs already climbed is for fools.

For those feverishly moving up the workplace ladder, stepping down is not an option. But their quizzical quest for ascendency does not mean a step down cannot actually be a step up. Though a less obvious truth, it is poignant and powerful nonetheless.

First, let me explain what I mean by "stepping down." In some instances, as alluded to above, it does mean relocating yourself within the organization to a less-senior, less-prominent, less-spotlighted role—a role you "demote" yourself into, even if it means *not* being the "head honcho," "top dog," or boss running the show. And yes, moves like this typically come with a reduced salary. This type of decision tends to make organization leaders scratch their heads and question why you would choose to step down.

In an article entitled "Stepping Back Down the Ladder," Barbara Mitchell says, "Unfortunately, many organizations put people in 'boxes' and have difficulty understanding that people who have been in executive positions can be satisfied taking a role in which they won't be in charge."[2] (The same holds true regardless of the level of position you hold within the organization.) Most employers are confounded when an employee relinquishes a position others may be gunning for. But their lack of understanding or confusion as to why you may decide to relegate yourself to a role beneath the level you have attained does not make your choice to do so a flawed one. Maybe you have come to the same conclusion as Alice in Lewis Carroll's Wonderland tale, who said, "I've got to get back to my right size." Sometimes stepping down is a matter of *rightsizing* yourself.

That's the manner of stepping down that I am speaking of—the type that helps you better align yourself with who you are, a repositioning that allows you to be truer to yourself, your gifts, and your talents. In other words, if you know in your heart you are meant to be a fourth grade teacher, if that is your destiny, you shouldn't stoop to be the president of the United States. It's a matter of knowing who you are and what position you would best thrive in.

Aesop's Fables are short stories that emphasize how changing circumstances do not change the nature of something or someone. Only an idiot, according to these fables, expects someone or something to be other than what it is by nature. It is foolish, for example, to believe a wolf in sheep's clothes is anything more than a wolf. Despite masquerading as a sheep, he is still a wolf through and through. If you put him in a pen filled with sheep, it's only a matter of time before he feasts on that fattened woolly flock.

If you try to be someone other than who you are, it is to your own detriment. The same is true when it comes to your career: you must align yourself with a role or position that allows you to be fully you. As Oscar Wilde, renowned author famous for his unconventional approach to life and writing, has said, "Be yourself; everyone else is taken." Quentin Crisp, writer and humorist known for his flamboyance, echoed the same sentiment when he said something similar in his book *How to Have a Lifestyle*: "In the end you only have one thing to offer the world that no one else can give, and that is yourself."[3]

Sometimes we find ourselves in a position we are not well suited for. So I say, never allow yourself to be pigeonholed into an occupation or position that does not allow *you* to be part of the equation. Any job that asks you to divorce from your true self is not the job for you. And sometimes taking a step down is the best way—maybe the only way—to put yourself in a role that allows you to be the best version of yourself.

What makes stepping down or stepping back such a challenging undertaking? Why is this a difficult pill for some to swallow? The answers may be different for everyone, but I think there are at least three common reasons:

- A *realization* that you are not the "right" person for the job and someone else is better suited for it. This is hard to admit, and it takes courage to acknowledge and act upon that awareness. Others may interpret it as an admittance that something is "wrong" about your situation or, worse, about you. For those who define themselves according to the position they hold, this can be especially difficult. Stepping down can be a blow to their ego.

- A *resistance* to change. Most of us prefer our comfort zone and an area of safety over skating on the edge. Taking an atypical, uncommon approach to your career, and making a move like this—deciding to go down, not up—is like exploring unchartered territory. No matter how you slice it, a choice like this separates you from what you've grown accustomed to.

- A *reluctance* to let go. To let go of what? Maybe the following: the idea that "success" is measured by having a fancier title, something sophisticated-sounding like Vice President, Senior Vice President, Executive Director, or, even better, Chief Executive or the belief that a better-paying position is the equivalent of career nirvana; or the idea that your job is your identity. Fortunately, it is possible to reinvent yourself—by first taking a step down—and not have your self-worth take a hit.

Jeff Lynn knew when it was time to step down. He cofounded and served as chief executive officer of Seedrs, an equity crowdfunding business that helps growth-oriented companies to raise capital. The company had just raised a significant round of venture capital (Series A) and had plans to accelerate their growth. And that's when Jeff realized a different kind of CEO was needed for this phase in the company's evolution, someone with a proven track record of running a high-growth business.

In his mind, stepping aside as CEO was not an admission of an inability to contribute to the organization but an acknowledgment he was not the right person for *that* job. After a period of self-introspection, moments spent inside a "walled garden," he understood he was not the "right person to take the company to its next stage." Here's how he expressed it in an article entitled "How Do You Know When It's Time to Step Down?": "Both in terms of experience, but also what I think I am good at and where I thrive, I could see that it would add a lot of value to the business to bring in a new CEO. But at the same time, I thought that there was a huge amount that I could still contribute to the business, and I never had an ego about titles."[4]

In short, Jeff *realized* he was not the "right" guy for the position, he did not *resist* the change that needed to happen, and it appears he had no *reluctance* in regard to letting go.

Part of tuning up your career is doing an assessment of whether or not you are best aligned with the role you occupy. Ask yourself the following questions: Does your position allow you to utilize your gifts and talents most fully? Are you frustrated in your job because the work you do feels like a "burden" and does not afford you the opportunity to do that which you excel at? Are you remaining in a role *only* because it pays the "big bucks"? If money were of no consequence and you had your druthers, would you put yourself in a different position, one that better aligns with who you are and what you truly enjoy doing?

Maybe you feel you are right where you need to be within the organization. Fantastic. More than likely, many of you are overdue for a checkup to determine if this part of your career engine—whether or not you are properly positioned within the company—is functioning as it should. If something feels off— you don't feel right being in the job you are in, you're fighting and resisting changes that need to be made, or you are staying in a role only because of the money, title, or recognition it affords, and you can't let that go—then my advice to you is this: consider stepping down to step up. Though unconventional, it's the type of counterintuitive approach that repositions you to be the best possible *you* while at work.

SPARK PLUGS

- Taking a step down is *not* the worst possible thing you can do career-wise.
- Every step on your career journey does not need to be in an upward trajectory. There are times a step down makes complete sense, especially if it helps you better align your true self with what you do for a living.
- There are plenty of reasons why it might be difficult to take a step down, including how others may interpret a move like that. There are three in particular that are common to all who choose to do so: realizing and admitting you are not right for the job you are in, a resistance to change, and a

reluctance to let go of the idea that somehow your success is contingent on title, salary, and position with a company. Stepping down or taking a step back could be a blow to one's ego.

- Take the time to assess where you are in your career to determine if your job duties are aligned with who you are and what you love to do.
- If your career is misaligned, list the areas that need to be fixed and think about corrective measures for them.

PART 3

MONEY MATTERS AND THE MATTER OF MONEY

8 THE TRANSFORMATIVE POWER
OF GOLD

THE BEST PART OF WORK IS THE PEOPLE; SADLY, THEY CAN also be the worst part.

You will find all types make up a workforce. Clint Eastwood would categorize them simply: the good, the bad, and the ugly. Their office names are more colorful: brown-noser, kiss-ass, whiner, team player, yeller and screamer, worker bee, backstabber, asshole, big cheese, pencil pusher, and bean counter, to name some. But there is one group at the office that is in a class by themselves: the money motivated.

One such person in a class by himself was Itzchak Tarkay—Israeli acrylic painter and watercolorist extraordinaire. At the age of nine, he and his family were sent during World War II to a Nazi concentration camp in Mauthausen, Austria, heartlessly hauled away to remote killing fields, where dreams were darkened, hopes faded into a black abyss, and lives were snuffed out like a candle's light. He and his family happened to be on "the list" of those to be exterminated, even though the existence of a list never entered their minds.

After being liberated by Allied forces in 1949—when light finally broke through the darkness—he immigrated to Israel, received a scholarship to the Avni Art Academy and learned from well-known Israeli artists of the time.

Influenced by French Impressionists and Post-Impressionists like Matisse and Toulouse-Lautrec, Tarkay's art focused on dream-like images of elegant women, perhaps in reaction to the heart-wrenching images he saw at Mauthausen. His paintings juxtapose and layer colors, allowing tones to bleed into each other in an atypical way, creating vibrant shades for the backgrounds, clothing, faces, and even the eyeshadow of the females he brings to life on canvas.

Despite years staring into a black abyss in one of life's darkest places, he still envisioned spectrums of color. He found a kaleidoscope of hues from which to paint and defied the blackness of his experience, letting radiant colors splash onto tarps waiting to be touched by his brush.

For such a virtuoso, his moniker as "a magician with color" could not have been more apt.

Unlike Tarkay, "money motivated" employees suffer from a strange type of color blindness, one which only allows them to see one color: gold. They may use various brushes to paint, like round and fan brushes, and they may utilize different stroke techniques, like blending and smudging, but upon their palette only *one* color sits and only *one* color makes it onto the canvas.

This class of people should not be confused with eager individuals who hustle and work their asses off, dedicated employees who go above and beyond the call of duty, who log overtime day in and day out and who toil to make some hard-earned cash to make a better life for themselves and their family. More power to them. They should be rewarded and then some for their efforts. As the sayings go, "The worker is worth her keep," and "We reap what we sow," although it should be noted, the dispensation of wealth can be strangely capricious, being showered upon both the lucky and the unlucky, the hardworking and the lazy, the righteous and the unrighteous alike. "It sometimes happens that one man has all the toil, and another all the profit," as Aesop reminds us in his *Fables*.[1]

Hardworking or not, when I discuss the "money motivated," I'm referring only to those who, like Gollum in Tolkien's *The Lord of the Rings*, are obsessed with Earth's most precious commodity. Once an average-looking Hobbit, Gollum's body and mind become deformed and twisted due to the corruption of "the Ring," an alluring and powerful circle of gold called "Precious" by its owners. This obsession eats away at him; he spends his days in a quenchless feud between a lust *for it* and a desire to be free *from it*.

The pages of Tolkien's book come to life at our places of work, where Gollum-like people walk among us bewitched by gold's charm, shackled by its attractiveness. Under its spell, all become crazed miners swept up in a Gold Rush frenzy. The prospect of finding it becomes their monomaniacal pursuit.

In June 2007 an American documentary television series called *American Greed* first premiered. Watch enough episodes and you'll realize greed's reach is extensive, spanning from the gutters of society to the hallowed halls of justice, from houses of ill repute to houses of worship, from mom-and-pop businesses to Wall Street's top money management firms. In a nutshell, the show highlights the great lengths taken by fixated "gold diggers" to screw people over for money: Ponzi schemes, embezzlement, white-collar crimes, money laundering, murder, and all kinds of fraud.

Some even marry for it.

Enter the drop-dead-gorgeous twenty-three-year-old who

marries the eighty-seven-year-old millionaire. She loves the man, so she says, but has something else caught her attention? At the marriage altar—where vows of love and fidelity are professed—she pledges eternal loyalty. Witnesses are left scratching their heads, wondering if deep down she loves him or what she hopes to obtain when he passes. Perhaps she seeks a "pot of gold"—a portfolio of assets at the end of a gold-bespeckled rainbow.

In the movie *The Ten Commandments*, director Cecile B. DeMille immortalizes a different kind of ceremony in which gold plays a prominent role. Moses goes up the mountain to receive the tablets of stone etched with the Lord's commands. The Israelites—who have questioned God throughout their desert wanderings—grow weary waiting on him. Impatient, they recruit Aaron, Moses's brother, to fashion an idol made of gold—a clear violation of commandment number two, which has already been communicated to them on different occasions. Aaron proceeds to fashion a golden cow and even constructs an altar in front of it so the Israelites can bow in reverence to it.

Once the altar is in place, the party starts.

And the hoopla reaches God's ears. Displeased, he tells Moses: "Go down, because your people, whom you brought up out of Egypt, have become corrupt. . . . [They] have made themselves an idol cast in the shape of a calf" (Exodus 32:7–8). When Moses reaches base camp, the Israelites are still "raising the roof"—singing and dancing before the idol, enraptured in its golden glow. Ignoring God's command regarding idol worship yet again, they are found prostrate before the inanimate object.

The Old Testament is replete with stories of God's fiery displeasure with those who bow to items crafted of metal, stone, or wood, and these stories almost always emphasize how idol worship corrupts the worshipper. Eventually, New Testament authors would equate greed—the selfish, extreme love of something like money—with being idolatrous. Their writings expand the definition of idolatry to include bowing to anything placed on the throne of one's heart. Apparently, the Israelites skipped class the day this commandment was taught and needed to learn its lesson again.

Money-crazed employees need a refresher course on the subject too: they are equally as beguiled by the luster of wealth as God's chosen were by the golden calf. Their actions prove their love for it; their appearance is smeared, splattered, and specked with it. As they hammer away fashioning their idol—a career hell-bent on making as much money as possible—wisps of gold leaflets rise and fall softly on their person, drawing attention like sparkling ornaments.

Years back, Disney's *Once Upon a Time* series caught my daughter's attention, and she cajoled the rest of the family to watch it with her. On a weekly basis we became involved in the lives of the fairy-tale characters—most borrowed from the Brothers Grimm and Hans Christian Andersen—who toggled between the real world and a fictional town called Storybrooke, where they resided.

The show yielded Disney $374.6 million over eight seasons. Some say Disney has the Midas touch with shows like this. (In Greek mythology, King Midas had the good fortune of turning whatever he touched into gold.)

The seasons that caught my eye focused on Rumpelstiltskin, the impish character who magically spins straw into gold—a much easier job than making bricks from straw, as the Israelites did while held captive in Egypt. In the show, Rumpelstiltskin is known as Mr. Gold, a powerful magician with a penchant for making deals. Jester-like movements, a prankish tone of voice, and a snickering laugh animate the mischievous and dubious nature of his character. And to match this sparkling personality,

Disney gives him a glistening golden complexion to highlight how gold dust has attached itself to him.

Some jobs are like that—they have a way of getting all over you: the mechanic who starts the day clean as a whistle but ends the day with hands, face, and clothes smeared with lubricant; the fry cook's apron gets oil splatters all over it; the baker's head, shoulders, knees, and toes become sprinkled with flour; and the white uniforms of those at Anthony's Pizzeria in Rockaway, New Jersey, where I grew up—a town resembling fictional Story-brooke—end up with polka dots of tomato sauce all over them.

These types of jobs tend to "paint" people, adding a pop of color to their uniforms. Other less noble "work"—deals done in secret with a wink and a nod, insider trades, corporate coup d'états, and other murky transactions—also leave their mark, not on clothes but on hearts and souls.

The darker the deed, the more striking the stain.

The Strange Case of Dr. Jekyll and Mr. Hyde by Robert Louis Stevenson illustrates the transforming effect work can have. The good doctor's scientific research, which bordered on the mystical, leads to the formulation of a homemade potion with the capacity to affect one's appearance and character. After ingesting it, Dr. Jekyll morphs into Mr. Hyde, his fiendish and murderous alter ego.

The story emphasizes the dual nature of humankind; within us lies both darkness and light, good and evil—and an inclination toward corruption. These two natures are at war within us —much like the battle that wages within Gollum—and it only takes a few sips of a prepared tincture, a concoction conjured in a lab, for the more sinister side to overtake the moral, well-intentioned side.

After his nights "on the sauce," Jekyll wakes with nasty hang-overs, leaving him to question whether he is more Jekyll than

Hyde or more Hyde than Jekyll. (A splitting headache coupled with a split personality seems a dreadful combination.) And the more he imbibes the cocktail, the more this dual existence becomes a concern. Eventually, Hyde's darker side dominates, and Jekyll's better nature recedes into a dark background.

Something similar happens to Anne Hathaway's character in *The Devil Wears Prada*. Andy, a recent college graduate with dreams the size of California, needs a job. She lands a gig at a prestigious fashion magazine, where she ends up being the assistant to Miranda Priestly, played by Meryl Streep.

Miranda—which in Latin means admired—is far from *admirable*. Dogmatic, demanding, and diabolical, she turns her new assistant into a whipping post and subjects her to a torturous initiation process.

Like Dr. Jekyll's potion, Miranda's influence eventually changes Andy. The elixir works its magic, transforming Andy into a different person. Her appearance and demeanor have been fashioned to befit someone working for a well-known fashion magazine. Only later does Andy grapple with how she has changed, after she mulls over who she was before the job and who she has become now that Miranda has her claws in her.

Those on the outside looking in, her boyfriend and close friends, see what Andy cannot: Miranda has imposed her own worldview on Andy. The more Andy drinks Miranda's "Kool-Aid," the more blind she becomes to her changing complexion. Her friends start seeing double: they can still see the selfless Jekyll-like Andy they know and love buried deep inside, but they also see the less-lovable Hyde-like Andy, hellbent on success at any price.

Those in your inner circle eventually see your shadowy side if you are chasing the almighty dollar too obsessively.

Work in secret all you want and hide behind the cover of

night, like Jekyll in his lab; avoid the light of day and linger in night's shadows as long as you can; but it's only a matter of time before a close friend catches a glimpse of who you've become. They will see the coating of gold makeup that leaves you glistening like Disney's Rumpelstiltskin.

No character in literature glistens from a love of money quite like Ebenezer Scrooge. In the initial chapters of *A Christmas Carol*, Dickens paints us a picture of a man insistent on acquiring and retaining wealth. Nothing else matters to him: not family, friends, or goodwill toward others. Even Christmas puts him off; he deems it a distraction to his money-making efforts. Preoccupied with his pursuit of gold, Scrooge ignores the *business* of charity, kindness, and forgiveness. One night, Scrooge's dead business partner, Jacob Marley, burdened by chains of greed and apathy toward others, visits him in a dream and delivers a warning. In soul-chilling fashion, he warns Scrooge about his avarice and tells him that he, too, wears chains—chains longer and heavier in weight than he had had seven years prior.

Scrooge pleads for comfort and mercy. Marley offers neither and vanishes, but not before telling him he will be visited by three Spirits. Each specter will attempt to convince Scrooge to abandon his greedy ways.

The Spirit of Christmas Past attempts to open Scrooge's eyes by reminding him of the person he used to be before the love of money took root within him. She takes him back to a time when he worked for Old Fezziwig, a boss overflowing with generosity. (Wealth held no sway over Fezziwig, and he took more pleasure in giving and sharing it with others than holding on to it.) During his apprenticeship with Fezziwig, Scrooge enjoyed a happy, carefree life. The lines of avarice were not yet painted on his face. The Spirit then proceeds to show Scrooge a moment when his golden pursuits began to flourish. A beautiful young lady cries as she sits by his side. She loves Scrooge but appears upset because, as she says, "another *idol* has displaced [her]" (italics mine). Clueless, Scrooge wonders what she means by this and asks what idol has *uprooted* her from the place of prominence in his heart. Her response minces no words: "A *golden* one" (italics mine). Then she adds, "I have seen your nobler aspirations fall off one by one, until the master-passion, Gain, engrosses you."[2]

Money-obsessed pursuits have costs associated with them; a price must always be paid. Scrooge sacrifices his love interest to cover the cost of obtaining the wealth he craves. But he also pays with his soul, like Faust, who makes a deal with the devil in Goethe's tragic play, exchanging his soul for unlimited material gain.

Although the Ghost of Christmas Past has removed some dirt from the windows of Scrooge's eyes and he sees the difference between his life then and now, he still needs convincing. As Marley has predicted, two other Spirits visit Scrooge overnight on Christmas Eve in an attempt to convert him.

Are Spirits on their way to visit you? Do you, like Scrooge, carry chains of greed and avarice?

Scrooge-like employees have dollar signs in their eyes, and a cha-ching ringtone echoes from their smartphone. (If you need a personalized money ringtone for your phone, I suggest the cash register sound from Pink Floyd's song "Money.") These wage earners care only about acquiring more wealth. Their goal is to take home the gold, "by hook or crook," as my mother says. Bronze and silver mean nothing; only a gold medal will do.

People go to great lengths to acquire riches, bartering fragments and pieces of themselves—a pulseless piece of their heart, a crusty corner of their soul, or a blackened bit of their brain—swapping them for fatter paychecks, bonuses, and stock options, as their nobler aspirations fall off one by one. And family and friends wonder where the person they once knew has gone.

My ramblings about gold—motivations to obtain it and its capability to corrupt—reminds me of the saying, "The love of money is a root of all kinds of evil"—an expression noted in Scripture (1 Timothy 6:10). Eight years of theological training will do this to you: verses you commit to memory haunt you like a ghost out of a Dickens novella.

This verse admonishes against having an insatiable thirst and hunger for money—the New Testament's equivalent of idolatry. In other words, an obsession with riches and wealth should never be your starting point. Nothing good follows from it. Keep that in mind as your career evolves.

Loved ones have told me that the dimples on my cheeks get more pronounced when I talk about closing deals. It appears I smile a lot when I make money. While some dimples are cute, this does not make for a pretty picture.

I hate to admit it, but I have been tarnished by a love of gold.

Like you, I hammer away at my job, striving to make as much money as I can, and without realizing it, I've become "gold plated." I guess when you are crazy in love, you are blind to everything else.

To acknowledge this is painful, but eight years of religious training also reminds me of the importance of confession. Plus, I would rather not be visited by Dickensian ghosts sent to address my redemption. It was best to change my ways before it came to that.

Sadly, somewhere along the way, I became Gollum, Hyde, Scrooge, even Faust.

Metamorphoses often happen gradually. Dr. Jekyll did not become Hyde by going on a drinking spree, binging his potion in a nonstop fashion: it all started with a few sips. Mr. Gold spins bits of straw into gold, not at a feverish pace but at a methodical one, tapping the loom's pedal like a drummer keeping the beat on a kick drum. Profit-crazed organizations never chant, "Chug, chug, chug," to get you to drink from its proverbial punch bowl. Instead, they escort you to it and encourage you to enjoy a ladleful because they know after one good taste, you will be back for more.

The following is a short story about taking a tiny taste and then wanting more.

Back in the day—I was fourteen at the time—I went on a drinking adventure with a buddy. On a sunny Sunday after-noon, we began to sip from a bottle of Cutty Sark, a god-awful scotch whiskey blend that tasted like turpentine. Not inclined to chug it, we passed the bottle back and forth—a sip for him, a sip for me.

Even though it tasted like crap, each sip convinced us to drink more.

Between swallows we carried on like foolish teenagers, acting like seasoned whiskey drinkers who knew how to appreciate "a real man's drink." Before long the bottle was empty. We consumed every drop—and the bottle consumed us. Who we were before our first sip had no resemblance to who we were after our last.

To this day I can only recall certain scenes: the initial couple swigs, a few chuckles with my buddy, stumbling to the house of another friend, and being carried home by my older brother and dad. (You know you are in bad shape when a sibling has no choice but to call Dad for help.) I was a mess.

My clothes did not fare any better either. Somewhere between stumbling from my friend's house and being carried home, I lost control of my bodily functions.

Yup!

I confess.

I did *it*.

Number two.

All over myself.

And remember, this all started with a sip.

It pains me to look back at this moment, as much as it pains Scrooge to see the less honorable moments in his past. I understand why Dr. Jekyll goes out of his way to *hide* Dr. Hyde, his fiendish darker side. It makes sense to me that Gollum lives in the middle of a lake deep inside the Misty Mountains; his obsession with "Precious" has turned him into a grotesque creature who prefers to keep his appearance hidden.

Once changed by the power of gold, Dr. Jekyll, Gollum, and Scrooge become tough to look at. Not even Tarkay, the "magician with color," could beautify that picture.

What if our painter's palette had more than one color on it? What if we blended gold with other colors? What if we painted with hues from the entire color wheel? What would the picture of our lives look like then?

If we did, Tarkay would be proud.

SPARK PLUGS

- Money-motivated people are a colorful bunch with one thing on their mind, getting their hands on as much money as possible.
- The love of money corrupts, and greed blinds us to all that truly matters.
- An obsession with money can develop gradually. Imperceptible at first, its effects are clear as day once it takes root. Usually someone close to you points out how you have changed.

- Money is not inherently bad; obsession with it is the problem.
- Something is always lost in a greedy pursuit of wealth: a price must be paid.
- A heart of gold is better than a pocket full of it.
- Ask yourself if money has changed you. Is gold the only color in your life?

9 A PARABLE: THE KING WHO HAD EVERYTHING AND NOTHING

Fairy tales about kings include castles. This story is no different.

Once upon a time, in a land far away but not far from our hearts, there lived a king who had everything and nothing at the same time.

Being a wealthy man, he denied himself nothing his heart desired. He commissioned artists to paint magisterial canvases to be hung in his castle. He acquired furniture crafted by artisans to furnish every room in his house: dining room tables, couches, chairs, curio cabinets, candleholders, custom-made wine racks, bookshelves, bedroom sets, and other fixtures that make a home beautiful. He bought countless items to fill every cupboard, cabinet, and compartment: books written by renowned authors; vases, ceramic bowls, dishes, cups, porcelain platters, and decanters made by potters; and utensils forged by craftsmen. He even procured trinkets, things of little importance or value, just because he could.

The king looked around and despite his castle being filled with countless possessions, he could not escape the thought that *something* was missing. "Ah," he said to himself, "The castle is cold, and I fear I'll catch a draft, get sick and die. I need rugs for every room!" So he ordered those in his employ—the maids, footmen, and majordomos—to acquire Persian rugs. And off they went, seeking woven floorcloths for the king. "If the king's feet are cold, his whole body will be cold," they said among themselves. "Oh dear! We can't have that," one said sarcastically.

Still, though every room had been adorned with plush carpets, a nagging feeling continued to gnaw at the king. His feelings of incompleteness puzzled him. "What more could I possibly need," the king pondered. "I know," he said. "I have not yet filled my cellar with the finest wines and brandies." Within days of returning from Persia, his servants were once again summoned and then sent to Italy and France to procure what was needed to fill his racks.

The king's workers returned with crate after crate of Bordeaux, Champagne, Burgundy, Chianti, Sangiovese, Montepulciano, Brunello, Barolo, Cognac, and Armagnac. The king then ordered them to remove every bottle from every crate and place them in the custom-made racks, each bottle assigned a place according to its region. No empty space could be found. "Now I can eat, drink, and be merry," the king exclaimed.

But merriment eluded the king, and a sense of hollowness hassled his heart. "Of course," the king chided himself. "I know what's missing! The closets are empty. I must fill them with the finest garments sold throughout the kingdom. My attire must reflect the full range of my power and mirror the full extent of my royalty! Even my headdress must express my kingliness," the king declared extemporaneously. (The king often imagined himself surrounded by others and spoke aloud as if others were listening.) Once again, he summoned his caretakers and dispatched them to buy pants, shirts, robes, undergarments, shoes, slippers, hats, and every imaginable accoutrement befitting a king, all made from the world's best silk, wool, cotton, and leather.

His attendants arranged for every garment, shoe, and hat to be placed in the king's closets. "There are enough clothes here to clothe ten kings," said one caretaker. "Maybe he's worried moths will eat some of them," another said. "How happy those moths would be to dine on such kingly attire," another jokingly added.

Finally, the king had filled his castle. "What an undertaking," the king said. "Now I have everything a king needs."

At the end of each day, however, an enigmatic emptiness filled him. "Maybe my eyes are deceiving me," he mused. So he surveyed each room to make sure each had a rug. He double-checked his wine cellar to prove to himself his racks were full. He opened every closet to ensure they were stuffed with clothes. And he examined every bookshelf, cabinet, and drawer to convince himself beyond a shadow of doubt that he had all he thought he had—and everything he thought he needed.

The king saw everything he had but saw not what he lacked.

As he was mulling this over, he heard laughter coming from the kitchen. The staff were brimming with enthusiasm and relishing each other's company. The kitchen bristled with happiness and contentment as they enjoyed a few moments together, recounting their travels while shopping for the king, satisfying his every whim. They joyously spoke of those they met at the art galleries, ateliers, vineyards, and haberdasheries. Despite the hard journey and long hours worked, they regaled themselves with lightheartedness, a feeling foreign to the king.

As the king sadly sauntered back to his bedchamber, he heard cheerful, playful sounds. Peering through a small window, he saw shabbily dressed children twirling and jumping in the castle's courtyard. Though upset to see them there—for how had they found their way into *his* courtyard?—he could not deny how merry they sounded. He momentarily reflected on the magical nature and innocence of playful children. A piercing pang punctured the king's heart as he contemplated how his childhood had lacked such whimsical pleasures.

Continuing upstairs, he heard celebratory noises echoing down the hall. Curious to learn the nature of this fanfare, he peered through another window and saw, just beyond the courtyard, several families gathered for a picnic. They appeared joyous in each other's company as they feasted on food from their gardens and farms—a simple reward for their hard work.

The king began pacing, troubled by these disquieting depictions of joy he had witnessed. Unsettled, he went to his study. Hoping to find peace as he basked in the shadow of his collection of famous literary works, a book grabbed his attention. *I've not read this one in some time*, he thought to himself. Flipping through its pages—which seemed guided by an invisible hand— he stopped, and a terse phrase caught his eye: "Uneasy lies the head that wears the crown."

Mesmerized and spellbound, melancholy and heavyhearted, he slouched on the ground.

"Uneasy is my soul and restless is my heart," cried the king. "But why is this so? I have everything a king could want and need. My castle is replete with worldly possessions curated for my pleasure and enjoyment."

The king who had everything felt a wretchedness deep in his spirit. For all his possessions—the artworks and books, the furnishings and clothes, the rugs and wine, every trinket, all the items in all the cabinets and drawers, and all the decorations perfectly placed on every shelf—he still felt empty. None offered solace for the burning heat of nothingness he felt in his soul.

Looking around, all he owned served only to highlight what he lacked. The king realized he had everything and nothing at the same time.

Alone and inconsolable, the king rued his existence. He had

never experienced the pleasure that others experienced, nor had his heart felt merriment and magic or the joy of family gatherings. His life was bereft of companionship, festiveness, and happiness.

The king had emptied his heart while filling his castle.

SPARK PLUGS

- There's nothing wrong with wanting more. The problem: being possessed by possessions.
- Remember: true wealth—and life itself—are not defined by what you have.
- Possessions are nice but will never satisfy your soul.
- Beware of greed in all its forms, especially toward wealth.
- The goal of your career is not to have a large bank account. Making money is what you do so you can have a life.

CONCLUSION

In the neighborhood where I grew up lived a man who had a fire-engine red Chevrolet Corvair parked in his driveway. It sat parked adjacent to the side of his house for as long as I can remember. I never once saw him drive the car.

I assumed something was wrong with it: a problem with the starter, fuel leaks, transmission failure—or worse, the engine was seized and needed replacing. Regardless, he kept the car, because, as he said, "It looks good and that's good enough for me."

Despite being young, I couldn't help but think, *Wouldn't it look better if you were in it cruising down the road?*

A parked car, no matter how old or new it might be, seemed contrary to the purpose of a car.

Maybe he didn't know how to fix it. Maybe, like me, he never ran the risk of being called a mechanic. Heck, I can't even change the oil in a car. Or maybe he couldn't afford to get it fixed. I know people who have spent thousands restoring old vehicles; finding compatible or original parts can cost an arm and a leg.

But most of what needs to be done is not too costly or difficult to do: change the oil and oil filter; check the lights, tires, and brakes; test the battery and replace it if needed; examine the suspension and steering alignment; and clean up the interior and exterior of the vehicle where required. Give the car a good wash and wax and she is road ready.

Too many people in the workforce are like my old neighbor. They seem content knowing they have a car; whether or not they take it for a ride is of no concern to them. And that's sad. That Corvair was made with so much more in mind. It was manufactured with the idea of getting you from one place to another and taking you wherever you want to go and even, some would say, looking cool in the process.

So the obvious question becomes, Where do you want to go career-wise, and how do you get from point A to point B in relation to your work life? After you answer that, you're expected to answer a corollary question: What are you willing to do to ensure your career engine functions optimally? Is some maintenance required for it to reach peak performance?

Tune Up Your Career has offered you a handful of ideas on where to start. The "tips" I recommend—taking ownership of your career, determining if you're meant to be an entrepreneur, viewing "wrong" moves differently, interpreting change properly, and considering stepping down to better align yourself with your career aspirations—are far from exhaustive, but they can at least get you started on cleaning out any gunk and goo your engine has accumulated over the last ten to twenty years. And it won't hurt either to reassess the importance of money to you and your motivations in obtaining it.

Whether or not you take the time to look under the hood and fix what needs fixing is up to you.

As the years went by, I moved away from the home I grew up in, in New Jersey. I went to college in Oklahoma and from there continued heading west and planted myself in sunny California. When I'd return to visit—during spring break, summer break, the holidays, and for other reasons—I would see that fire-engine red Corvair still parked in the driveway. As a person who appreciates the journey and getting from one place to another and enjoying the ride while doing it—whether in one's career or life in general—it was a sad sight to see. That baby needs to be taken for a spin.

APPENDIX A

TUNE UP YOUR CAREER CHECKLIST

At the end of this book on tuning up your career, I thought it might be useful to collect its concepts in one place. You will find some to be abstract and others more concrete. They represent fundamental wisdom for career improvement that I have learned over thirty years of finding jobs for people. When your career engine feels sluggish, refer to this list.

Chapter 1 - Mice, Mazes, and Manchego

- Sometimes being an employee feels like you are a mouse in a maze looking for cheese. Everyone is on the hunt for "cheese," rewards that make it all worthwhile.
- Work circumstances change all the time, making it hard to find and secure those rewards. Your survival depends on your ability to adapt to those changes.
- Changing circumstances create opportunities.

- Don't forget that work "mazes" contain traps. Watch your step.
- It's possible to lose yourself as you navigate through the maze; stay true to yourself.

Chapter 2 - Welcome to the Machine

- When it comes to work, it's easy to feel like you are just part of "the machine," a heartless system that's grinding away at your individuality.
- Some companies foster individuality; others stifle it in favor of a more homogenized approach to their business.
- Understand that business in general is guided by capitalism and the main concern of an employer is the bottom line on their profit-and-loss statement.
- The best employer to work for is the one who values who you are and allows you to be yourself and use your gifts in a way that contributes to the growth of the company.

Chapter 3 - Take Ownership of Your Career

- The antidote to career complacency and dissatisfaction is taking ownership of it. Reliance on others to develop your career is an unwise strategy.
- A career engine never runs right if the individual has not taken full responsibility for it.
- Taking ownership of your career does two things: it gives you control and makes you responsible for how it turns out. Control and responsibility are two sides of the same coin.

- Remember: personal accountability is the foundation of every noteworthy career.
- In mythology, the story of Orestes shows that curses turn to blessings once a person takes responsibility for what has happened in his or her life. Pointing the finger at people and problems prevents progress.

Chapter 4 - Don't Look Now, but You May Be an Entrepreneur

- Entrepreneurship is career ownership at the highest level, but it is not a road easily traveled.
- Entrepreneurs are people who "go for it." There's no magic formula, no silver bullet, no overnight success, no hocus pocus, and no waving of a wand. It's about starting *somewhere* and having the guts to do everything in your power to make *something* happen.
- If you choose this path, remember the following: do not despise small beginnings, accept failure as part of the process, wait for the right moment, and use your intuition.

Chapter 5 - Wrong Moves Are Not Final Moves

- All steps on a career journey are interconnected. Last steps on one road are connected to the first steps on another. Every step and perceived misstep has led to where you are.
- Any "wrong" move you think you have made is not a "final" move.
- Careers are a cluster of characteristics that include

right and wrong moves, steps and missteps, and ground gained and sometimes lost.

- The only thing that matters is your response to your perceived "wrong" move. Don't let your career be governed by moves already made, whether you think they were right or wrong.
- Remain open to new directions your career may take. Do not be so wedded to your preconceived ideas about your career that you fail to see the golden opportunity right before your eyes.

Chapter 6 - The Tea Leaves in the Bottom of the Cup

- How you interpret change is essential to your career engine functioning at its best.
- New developments and unexpected events—in other words, change—happen at work all the time. Learning how to read those changes and adapt to them is critical.
- You will be better positioned to retain control of your career if you get better at recognizing the "signs" of change.
- Here are some things you can do when change is on the horizon: assess your career progress, decide if you can live with the impending change, plan an exit if you cannot, and expect there to be a period of adjustment either way.

Chapter 7 - A Step Down Can Be a Step Up

- A big career misconception is this: taking a step down is the worst thing you can do.

- Most believe you should only ascend a corporate ladder. Our career trajectory should always be upward.
- Remember: it is to your own detriment when you try to be someone other than yourself.
- Though unconventional, stepping down is a counterintuitive yet often effective approach to reposition yourself so you can be the best *you* at work.

Chapter 8 - The Transformative Power of Gold

- People motivated solely by money are a colorful bunch with one thing on their mind: getting their hands on as much of it as they can.
- The problem is not the desire to make as much money as you can. Rather, it is the love of money that is the issue. Money is not inherently bad. The obsession with it is.
- There is always a price to pay in any greedy pursuit of wealth.
- Better a heart of gold than a pocketful of it.

Chapter 9 - A Parable: The King Who Had Everything and Nothing

- There's nothing wrong with wanting more. Being possessed by possessions is another thing altogether.
- Beware of greed in all its forms, especially a lust for wealth.

APPENDIX B
RECOMMENDED READING

Aesop. (1484) 1968. *Aesop's Fables.* New York: Nelson Double-day, Inc.

Armstrong, Karen. *A Short History of Myth.* New York: Canongate Books, 2005.

Bly, Robert. *Iron John: A Book About Men.* Boston: Da Capo Press, 1990.

Briskin, Alan. *The Stirring of the Soul in the Workplace.* San Francisco: Jossey-Bass Publishers, 1996.

Bulfinch, Thomas. *Bulfinch's Mythology: The Age of Fable, The Age of Chivalry, Legends of Charlemagne.* New York: Random House, Modern Library Edition, 1993.

Cain, Susan. *Quiet: The Power of Introverts in a World That Can't Stop Talking.* New York: Crown Publishers, 2012.

Campbell, Joseph. *The Hero with a Thousand Faces*. Princeton, NJ: Princeton University Press, 1973.

Cervantes. *Don Quixote*. New York: Vikings Press International Collectors Library, 1951.

Crisp, Quentin. *How to Have a Lifestyle*. New York: Methuen, 1975.

Huxley, Aldous. *The Doors of Perception*. New York: First Harper Perennial Modern Classics, 2009.

Huxley, Aldous. *Brave New World*. New York: First Harper Perennial Modern Classics, 2010.

Iger, Robert. *The Ride of a Lifetime: Lessons Learned from 15 Years as CEO of the Walt Disney Company*. New York: Random House, 2019.

Isaacson, Walter. *Steve Jobs*. New York: Simon and Schuster, 2011.

Johnson, Spencer. *Who Moved My Cheese?* New York: G.P. Putnam's Sons, 1999.

Johnson, Spencer. *Peaks and Valleys: Making Good and Bad Times Work for You—At Work and in Life*. New York: Atria Books, 2009.

Keen, Sam. *Fire in the Belly: On Being a Man*. New York: Bantam Books, 1992.

Knight, Phil. *Shoe Dog: A Memoir by the Creator of Nike.* New York: Scribner, 2016.

Krass, Peter, ed. *The Book of Business Wisdom: Classic Writings by the Legends of Commerce and Industry.* New York: John Wiley and Sons, 1997.

Melville, Herman. *Moby Dick; Or, The Whale.* New York: Harper and Brothers, 1851.

Obama, Barack. *A Promised Land.* New York: Crown, 2020.

O'Connor, Ian. *The Captain: The Journey of Derek Jeter.* Boston: Houghton Mifflin Harcourt, 2011.

Parcells, Bill. *Finding a Way to Win: The Principles of Leadership, Teamwork, and Motivation.* New York: Doubleday, 1995.

Pollan, Stephen M., and Mark Levine. *Die Broke: A Radical, Four-Part Financial Plan to Restore Your Confidence, Increase Your Net Worth, and Afford You the Lifestyle of Your Dreams.* New York: HarperBusiness, 1997.

Riley, Pat. *The Winner Within: A Life Plan for Team Players.* New York: Berkley Books, 1993.

SHOUT-OUTS

Achievements are seldom solo efforts, and that is especially true when it comes to this book.

The messes in the original manuscript—awkward-sounding sentences, the improper use of grammar, and unclear paragraphs and transitions—were cleaned up by Deb Hall with Illumify Media. She is an editing and writing tutor of the first order. The book is better because of her.

Without my family and friends I would be a rudderless ship sailing vast seas. Something about each person—and a combination of them—helps me stay the course and maneuver through life's waters.

NOTES

Introduction

1. Herman Melville, *Moby Dick Or The Whale* (1851; New York: Random House, 1992), 230.

1. Mice, Mazes, and Manchego

1. Spencer Johnson, *Who Moved My Cheese?: An A-mazing Way to Deal with Change in Your Work and in Your Life* (New York: G.P. Putnam's Sons, 1999), 25.
2. Spencer Johnson, *Who Moved My Cheese?*, 26.
3. Spencer Johnson, *Who Moved My Cheese?*, 32.
4. Ram Charan, *The Attacker's Advantage: Turning Uncertainty into Breakthrough Opportunities* (Philadelphia, PublicAffairs, 2015), 31.
5. Cervantes, *Don Quixote* (New York: Vikings Press International Collectors Library, 1951), 514.
6. Tess Vigeland, *Leap: Leaving a Job with No Plan B to Find the Career and Life You Really Want* (New York: Harmony Books, 2015), 118.
7. *Harry Potter and the Goblet of Fire*, directed by Mike Newell, written by Steve Kloves and J.K. Rowling (Burbank, CA: Warner Bros. Pictures, 2005).

3. Take Ownership of Your Career

1. Walter Isaacson, *Steve Jobs* (New York: Simon and Schuster, 2016), page 186, 194–99.

4. Don't Look Now, but You May Be an Entrepreneur

1. Ben Brody, "11 Inspiring Tales of Unexpected Success," *Westchester Magazine*, January 27, 2012, https://westchestermagazine.com/life-style/business/11-inspiring-tales-of-unexpected-success.
2. Tess Vigeland, *Leap: Leaving a Job with No Plan B to Find the Career and Life You Really Want* (New York: Harmony Books, 2015), 43.

3. Peter Krass, ed., *The Book of Business Wisdom: Classic Writings by the Legends of Commerce and Industry* (New York: John Wiley and Sons, 1977), 366–67.
4. Peter Krass, ed., The Book of Business Wisdom, 367.

5. Wrong Moves Are Not Final Moves

1. Stephen R. Covey, *The 7 Habits of Highly Effective People* (New York: Simon and Schuster, 1989), 91.
2. Tess Vigeland, *Leap: Leaving a Job with No Plan B to Find the Career and Life You Really Want* (New York: Harmony Books, 2015), 135.

6. The Tea Leaves in the Bottom of the Cup

1. Ken Rosenthal, "'Help Me Fix This': Inside Matt Carpenter's Cross-Country Quest to Remake His Swing,"TheAthletic.com, February 23, 2022, https://theathletic.com/3142459/2022/02/23/help-me-fix-this-inside-matt-carpenters-cross-country-quest-to-remake-his-swing/.
2. Robert Iger, *The Ride of a Lifetime: Lessons Learned from 15 Years as CEO of the Walt Disney Company* (New York: Random House, 2019), 230.

7. A Step Down Can Be a Step Up

1. Tess Vigeland, *Leap: Leaving a Job with No Plan B to Find the Career and Life You Really Want* (New York: Harmony Books, 2015), 125.
2. Barbara Mitchell, "Stepping Back Down the Ladder," The Center for Association Leadership, accessed October 11, 2022, https://www.asaecenter.org/association-careerhq/career/articles/job-search-strategies/stepping-back-down-the-ladder.
3. Quentin Crisp, *How to Have a Lifestyle* (New York: Methuen, 1975), 8.
4. "How Do You Know When It's Time to Step Down?", Seedrs.com, accessed October 12, 2022, https://www.seedrs.com/academy/how-do-you-know-when-its-time-to-step-down-as-founder-ceo/.

8. The Transformative Power of Gold

1. Aesop, *Aesop's Fables* (New York: International Collectors Library, 1968), 118.
2. Charles Dickens, *A Christmas Carol* (New York: Random House-The Modern Library, 1995), 45.

ABOUT THE AUTHOR

Chris Fontanella is the founder of Encore Professionals Group, a professional services firm specializing in the identification and placement of accounting and finance candidates in temporary and regular, full-time positions.

He previously served as Division Director for Robert Half International and Client Service Director for Resources Global Professionals.

Prior to entering the staffing industry, he spent years studying theology and preparing for ministry, having received his bachelor of arts degree in New Testament Studies from Oral Roberts University and his master of arts degree in Theological Studies from Fuller Theological Seminary.

Chris is also the author of *Jump Start Your Career: Ten Tips to Get You Going*, which offers foundational thoughts and ideas for those about to start their career.

Chris continues to provide staffing services through Encore while he explores the world of writing and publication.

Lightning Source UK Ltd.
Milton Keynes UK
UKHW010650270123
416064UK00004B/370

9 781959 099079